What Leaders Are Saying About the *Power To Create* curriculum . . .

I am so excited about the *Power to Create* curriculum. Tim excellently teaches there is a purpose for you succeeding in life.

Dr. John Bevere,
Messenger Intl, Bestselling Author

This curriculum is chalked full of wisdom and information that will literally bring about a true transformation.

Simon T. Bailey,
Speaker of the Year by Meeting Professionals Intl

The *Power To Create* curriculum will not only change you, but it will change those around you.

Dr. Robb Thompson,
Pastor & International Speaker

Tim Redmond's material is outstanding! I encourage you to get a hold of it and work it like a gold mine.

Dr. Lance Wallnau,
Transformation Expert, 7 Mountains Specialist

Many Christians have a great relationship with the King but don't understand Kingdom principles . . . This is where Tim Redmond is an expert. He's dynamic, riveting and I highly recommend him.

Brian Klemmer,
Breakthrough Specialist

God placed something on the inside of you that He thought the world should not do without. This powerful curriculum will place a demand on your potential and truly bring global impact.

Dr. Joseph Ripley,
Pastor, Body of Christ Church Int'l

I have seen Tim in the local church – he adds a tremendous amount of value to what the pastor is trying to accomplish.

Mike Rovner,
Multimillionaire Entrepreneur

Tim Redmond addresses the subject of Biblical economics and finances from a tremendous balance. Tim is a great communicator and his insights are stellar. I recommend him highly.

Pastor Dennis Slavens,
Antioch Church

Tim Redmond has the most amazing gift set for taking your life to the next level in business, ministry and whatever God has called you to.

Jerry Horst,
Commercial and Residential Developer

TIM REDMOND

POWER TO CREATE

Unlock Greater Purpose, Relationships & Finances

Interactive Workbook & Journal

Power To Create Interactive Workbook & Journal
Unlock Greater Purpose, Relationships, and Finances
© 2011 by Tim Redmond, Redmond Leadership Institute

ISBN 978-1-890900-56-4

Product Development and Creative Consultants: Mike Loomis, www.vaughnstreet.com

Cover: Christian Ophus, www.eureka7.com

For further information, please contact:
Tim Redmond
Redmond Leadership Institute
PO Box 703052
Tulsa, OK 74170
918.298.7766
www.PowerToCreate.org

Printed in Canada

Table of Contents

POWER TO CREATE

Unlock Greater Purpose, Relationships & Finances

Getting Started . . .

Welcome! We are so honored and excited that you have decided to invest in this curriculum and even more so, into the amazing gift God has entrusted to you.

Prepare to take a journey of transformation by using ALL of the elements of the *Power To Create* package. This Workbook is designed to complement the video and audio sessions provided in the curriculum. All these materials have been carefully and prayerfully designed to help you understand what true wealth is and enable you to further develop your gift to significantly help others and glorify God.

This interactive Workbook is easy to follow. You can go through it at your own pace, by yourself, or with others. Some suggestions for this curriculum study are below, but choose whatever way works best for you.

There are eight DVD sessions, each packed with teaching and inspiring stories. Each video session begins with "Interviews on the Street" to alert your thinking, continues on to my presentation to provide you with powerful teaching, and concludes with a "Leadership Lesson" based on a thematic scene to reinforce the key concepts into your memory.

For instance, the first session is called "The Mess" and the Leadership Lesson recap was filmed at the biggest mess in Tulsa—the city dump!

There are also eight CD sessions with audio versions from the material on the DVDs, so you can enjoy this curriculum in your home or on the go!

Workbook chapters correspond to the audio and video sessions on the CDs and DVDs. For example, the material covered on Session One of the CD and DVD complements the material in Session One of this book. We recommend that you go through this book in a step-by-step process as you watch the corresponding DVD sessions.

Here are some of the special features of this Workbook that will maximize your learning experience:

❑ *PowerKeys* — These create expectation in your mind and heart for what will be covered in the session.

❑ *Companion Exercise to the Video* — As you watch the videos, fill in the blanks on ten key thoughts covered at the beginning of each chapter.

❑ *My Notes from the Video Session* — Keep all of your learning experiences in one convenient place—here in this workbook! As you watch each video session, take notes in the space provided.

❑ *Personal Discovery* — This is where the heart of your learning occurs. The material is explained and combined with innovative activities to practically apply it to your life.

❑ *Personal Application* — What are you going to do with all of the powerful principles provided in each session? This section gives you a practical way to produce results with what you learn.

❑ *Between You and God* — Pray this anointed prayer to invite God to be intimately involved in your transformation.

❑ *Capturing Your Learning* — What did you learn and experience during each session? What is the Lord saying to you? This section gives you room to capture the value you received and journal it in your own words.

❑ *Corridor of the Experts* — Tap into the wisdom of the experts Tim has assembled to strengthen and expand your understanding of the material, and take notes on the expert teaching in this section. Access the expert clips at the www.PowerToCreate.org Web site.

As you go through this Workbook, take time to write down your thoughts, questions, ideas, and notes from the material. The more you engage with this material, the more your life will be transformed.

Guard against the temptation of just being a spectator. Involve your heart and life into the learning activities. As James said, "But be doers of the word, and not hearers only, deceiving yourselves" (James 1:22). Your writing is an effective way of being a "doer of the word" and will lead to better results in your life.

Personal Study Tips

Watch each video session with a pen in hand and your Workbook open.

Enjoy the sessions. Be flexible in how you go through the materials in this curriculum. You may prefer to watch a DVD session several times, completing the Workbook gradually while soaking up the material. Reinforce your learning by listening to the CDs while driving in your car or working around the house.

The curriculum is designed for you to complete one chapter each week, but you can take it at your own pace. Whether you are working through this curriculum on your own or with a group, take a few minutes each day to complete a portion of the Workbook.

Consistency is the key! Decide on a workable schedule to complete the sessions, then keep it *faithfully*.

Journaling

One of the features of this interactive study is times of "journaling"— writing down your thoughts and impressions as your journey through the Workbook.

Webster's dictionary[1] defines *journal* as "a record of experiences, ideas, or reflections kept for private use." You can see from this definition that everyone can "journal," even if you've never done it before.

Here are some guidelines to assist you as you journal:

❏ Follow the instructions for each journaling portion, and take time to enjoy this exercise.

❏ Combine personal honesty with prayer as you respond to the questions and journaling sections.

❏ Expect your Creator to breathe life into you as you study, reflect, and take action!

Group Study

If possible, before group sessions, find out how your group leader wants to organize the sessions. You may be asked to complete the video and workbook chapter before each session or to wait and go through it with your group.

Your group leader will provide answers when needed and facilitate discussions in each session.

As you attend each session, be open when sharing what you have learned and encourage others as they share. Remember that this group study is not a time for personal counsel or advice. Respect each participant, and trust that God is leading him or her.

To help facilitate and promote group study, download the *Power to Create Leader's Guide* available at www.PowerToCreate.org.

We have included specific questions and topics for discussion in the Leader's Guide.

---

[1] *Merriam-Webster's Collegiate Dictionary Eleventh Edition.* Copyright © 2003 by Merriam-Webster, Incorporated.

POWER TO CREATE

Unlock Greater Purpose, Relationships & Finances

*. . . for it is he who
gives you the ability
to produce wealth . . .*

—Deuteronomy 8:18 NIV

Session 1
The Mess

PowerKeys

❏ God has given us a tremendous gift that has not be recognized or valued by many because of the confusion surrounding the topic of wealth.

❏ Because of bad examples and experiences, many have negative associations regarding wealth and finances.

❏ This gift needs to be redefined to understand what God had in mind when He gave it to us.

Companion Exercise for Video Session 1

1. The love of money is the root of all evil; poverty is the _____ of all evil.

2. Deuteronomy 8 is more of a _____ chapter than a blessing. It is a call to remember the Lord your God—don't forget Him!

3. In Deuteronomy 8:18 it says, "For it is He who gives you power to get wealth." The word to "get" actually means to _____.

4. Kingdom-based wealth has more to do with purpose and relationships than _____.

5. Wealth comes from the word "_____," which affects all aspects of your life, much like the Hebrew word for *peace* (*shalom*).

6. In the same way we have relationships with people, we also have a relationship with _____ and _____.

7. Many times, the reason we go negative when thinking about wealth and money is because we have a _____ relationship with it.

8. Out of a fear of making sure we don't love money, we don't respect it. Whatever we disrespect, we _____ out of our lives.

9. We should pursue our _____, not our results.

10. Kingdom-based wealth _____ what the world pursues.

My notes from Video Session 1:

My notes from Video Session 1:

Personal Discovery

In Deuteronomy 8:18, "to get" actually means "to create or produce."

In other words, God's focus on this gift is creating, not getting.

What's the difference between creating and getting?

> *And you shall remember the LORD your God, for it is He who gives you power to get wealth, that He may establish His covenant which He swore to your fathers, as it is this day.*
>
> **Deuteronomy 8:18**

_____

_____

_____

In your life, what areas have you been more focused on "getting" than "creating"?

_____

_____

_____

_____

Whom Are You Serving?

God's Kingdom is focused on serving others. The world's thinking is primarily self-centered. This is the major contrast between these two kingdoms and economic systems.

Through which lens are you looking at "wealth"? One lens looks at it very positively because it is focused on others. The other lens will blur your image of wealth because it is focused on putting yourself before others.

This is where much of the confusion has crept into people's thinking on this topic. If you look at something with the wrong lens, you won't be able to see and understand it clearly. Since most people equate wealth with money, we're closely examining the topic of money in this segment.

In Video Session 1, I stated, "When we despise or don't understand a gift God gives us, we rob ourselves of the power that gift was designed to bring into our lives."

What does that mean to you?

_____

_____

How could this be affecting you today?

_____

_____

When you think of the word "wealth" what do you see? Write or draw what comes to mind:

Trivial Pursuits

How you view things—your internal images—significantly influences the results in your life. The more accurate and powerful your images become, the better the results.

Let's start with how "wealth" is commonly defined: a large store or accumulation of money, property, or valuable possessions.

Without understanding God's intention, many have pursued "getting" money, property, and possessions at the cost of their peace and joy. Something is wrong with that picture.

You are defined by what you pursue.

You are defined by what you pursue.

Do you have the right images of wealth? Are you pursuing the right thing?

In looking honestly at your life, what have been your top three pursuits? (In other words, in what and in whom have you invested the most time, energy, and money?)

1. _____

2. _____

3. _____

Consider the state of affairs both in our culture and around the world.

The lives of many are ruled by a tremendous level of anxiety and fear—especially on the subject of finances.

Why do YOU think there is so much fear and anxiety associated with money?

_____

_____

_____

The Mess

To understand this mess, we will first talk about relationships . . .

Think of a good relationship you have had. Can you picture that person now?

What words or feelings come to mind when you think of this relationship?

Now imagine a bad relationship you have had.

What words or feelings come to mind when you think of this relationship?

Just as we have relationships with people, we also have a relationship with wealth and money.

Our relationship with money can be described with the same words, phrases, or feelings we use to describe our good and bad relationships.

How would you describe your relationship with money, both positively and negatively?

Positive: _____

_____

_____

Negative: _____

_____

_____

Have you ever heard about a person who was ruined by suddenly acquiring a large sum of money through an inheritance, retirement, settlement, or lottery?

Leaders are interested in the true cause and effect of these situations. What was the real reason for that person's life being messed up by money?

Did money *ruin* them . . . or did it just *reveal* what was already there? Money magnifies what is in the hearts of people, whether good or bad.

Did money ruin them . . . or did it just reveal what was already there?

Yet if one believes that money ruins people, what kind of relationship will that person have with money?

Imagine you are given ten million dollars today. Based on your past relationship with money, what areas would be magnified in your life? (Would the results be good or bad?)

_____

_____

_____

Many of the internal scripts and beliefs you carry today were formed when you were a child. Think of all the influences in your life growing up—your parents, family, friends, teachers, pastors, and even media figures.

While growing up, what I heard and saw about money was (answer below):

1.
2.
3.
4.
5.
6.
7.

Most people are unaware of how the beliefs of those close to them have shaped their thinking. Your responses above are worth serious consideration.

Most of us desire to honor God in the way we live and think. We read scriptures that warn us about trusting in riches. We hear of people's lives falling apart, and we inaccurately give the reason why by misquoting 1 Timothy 6:10, saying that "money is the root of all evil." (The verse actually says, "The *love* of money is the root of all evil [emphasis added]).

Please respond—My greatest fears and concerns about being rich are:

1.
2.
3.
4.
5.
6.
7.

How are these affecting your daily life, career, and thoughts about money?

_____

_____

_____

Dangerous Myths

Much of what we believe about wealth and money is more myth than truth. The key is to replace wrong beliefs about wealth with the truth!

Here are some of the typical responses I hear from attendees of my *Power To Create* live seminars around the world:

- ❏ You can't be rich and spiritual.
- ❏ I am afraid riches will cause me to lose my passion for God.
- ❏ Money is the root of all evil.
- ❏ Rich people are greedy, covetous, or criminals.
- ❏ Money doesn't buy happiness.
- ❏ Not everyone can be rich.
- ❏ The rich get richer and the poor get poorer—it's not fair!
- ❏ There is never enough.

Take a moment and circle the statements above that reflect beliefs you have had or still have.

Should you be concerned about guarding your heart from being absorbed with the wrong focus? Absolutely!

- ■ Are the beliefs listed above helping or hurting me?
- ■ Are these beliefs resulting in good things being created?
- ■ Are these beliefs making the lives of those around me better?

Respond to the three questions above:

_____

_____

_____

Out of a fear of making sure we don't love money, we don't respect it. Whatever we disrespect, we devalue and drive out of our lives.

Experiences Shape Beliefs

We often have deep-seated negative beliefs about money and wealth because we may have seen:

❏ Our parents and family fight over money

❏ Destroyed marriages and businesses due to financial conflicts

❏ Betrayals of close relationships over money

❏ Our own bad experiences with money

Because of the negative experiences of our past AND the conclusions we have made based on those experiences, we may have created a negative relationship with wealth and money. Because of that, we may be consciously or subconsciously pushing it out of our lives.

A negative relationship with wealth and money can cause us to live from a place of . . .

❏ Selfishness

❏ Disempowerment

❏ Feeling and acting incapable

❏ Impossibility; a belief that we can't do it

In light of the truth that God gave us the power to create wealth and having a positive, healthy relationship with wealth and money (with a mindset to serve others) will help us live from a place of . . .

❏ Generosity

❏ Confidence

❏ Feeling and acting capable

❏ Possibility; that we can do it!

On a scale of 1-10, with 10 being the best, how healthy is your current relationship with money? (Please circle.)

1   2   3   4   5   6   7   8   9   10

Since God has given us a gift—the power to create wealth—we should remove and replace contradictory and self-sabotaging beliefs about wealth. Otherwise, we will be as Jesus stated in Mark 3:26, a house divided against itself that cannot stand.

Mastering Money

Once when addressing a group of people, most of whom were involved in business in some way, Jesus made a dramatic statement: "And if you are untrustworthy about worldly wealth, who will trust you with the true riches of heaven?" (Luke 16:11 NLT).

Here is the "Tim's paraphrased version" of this verse: "If you haven't mastered the money system on earth, how can God trust you with the true riches of heaven?"

Based on the verse above, how would you rate your "trustworthiness" regarding money? Why?

_____

_____

_____

Jesus is calling us to gain mastery over the money system rather than being controlled by it. He is calling us to have a healthy relationship with wealth and money rather than associating negativity with it.

What some people believe about wealth and money in the deepest part of their being is tied to fear, pain, misunderstanding . . . and yet . . . God has given us the power to create wealth.

How can that be? When we take this sacred, purpose-centered, God-given gift and collide it with the negative beliefs we may have regarding wealth and money, it creates an internal conflict.

This conflict is causing a mess!

Yet Proverbs 4:23 says to guard your heart with all diligence for out of it flow the issues of life. A respected Rabbi once shared with me that this is really saying, "For out of your heart you determine the borders of your possibilities."

Pause and consider that phrase, "the borders of your possibilities." What does that mean in your life, especially in regard to your thinking about wealth and money?

_____

_____

_____

Much More than Money

From a Kingdom perspective, there is much more to wealth than just obtaining possessions.

Money is a result; it should never be our pursuit. When it becomes our pursuit, it actually weakens us.

We should pursue our purpose (serving others in significant ways) instead of running on the hamster wheel chasing results. Chasing the wrong thing leaves our heart full of fear and anxiety—which is just the opposite of the peace and joy found in the Kingdom of God. (See Romans 14:17.)

Taking an honest and objective look at your history regarding money, what evidence of wrong thinking or wrong pursuits shows in your life?

_____

_____

_____

Whatever we pursue, we serve in some way.

In pursuing success, many make the mistake of chasing money instead of letting it chase them.

Whatever we pursue, we serve in some way.

Our pursuit should be our purpose. The world system seeks money, position, fame, more possessions. Yet Jesus says when we seek first God's Kingdom (which means becoming really good at serving others), all of these things are added to us. (See Matthew 6:33.)

A Bad Leader

Money is not bad in itself; it is neutral. It takes on the nature of the holder.

Money is actually the reward of the Kingdom-based wealth process and provides an opportunity for us to demonstrate stewardship and good choices. Money is a great follower but a bad leader. When money leads, it corrupts and invites deceit.

When money follows wealth, we enjoy riches without sorrow (based on Proverbs 10:22).

When money follows wealth, we enjoy riches without sorrow (based on Proverbs 10:22).

In the context of this study, Kingdom-based wealth has more to with purpose and relationships than finances (yet we don't disregard the importance of finances).

If you thought of "wealth" as being more focused on purpose and relation-ship-building than finances, how would the way you look at it change?

_____

_____

_____

_____

True wealth, Kingdom-based wealth, attracts what the world pursues.

Do you think you are pursuing money? What makes you think your response is true?

_____

_____

_____

_____

What is your heart really pursuing?

_____

_____

_____

_____

In future sessions, we are going to drill down much deeper into the many facets of wealth. But before we do, let us focus on God's design for the Church.

The Church is designed to be the most effective organization on the planet to . . .

❏ Help the hurting

❏ Provide powerful solutions to difficult problems

❏ Serve as a leadership development center that maximizes the God-given gifts and potential within people

❏ Take territory in one of the seven spheres of influence God is calling it to transform:

1. Family

2. Religion/Church

3. Business and Technology

4. Media

5. Education

6. Government

7. Arts, Sports, and Entertainment

This is where you move to center stage. Do you also realize that YOU are the Church?

An Excellent Spirit

God's design is to work intimately with and through you to reach compelling levels of excellence and influence.

The prophet Daniel illustrated this in his life and serves as a pattern for us to follow today. "Then this Daniel distinguished himself above the governors and satraps, because an excellent spirit was in him; and the king gave thought to setting him over the whole realm" (Dan. 6:3).

The Hebrew word for "excellent" means "exceeding" and "to be preeminent." It paints a picture of being the tallest peak that stands above the others around it. This is an ability to produce solutions that cause you to stand out and gain great influence in the area of your assignment, just as Daniel did.

> *This man Daniel . . . was found to have a keen mind (same Hebrew word for excellent) . . . and solve difficult problems. Call for Daniel . . . (Dan. 5:12 NLT, emphasis added).*

"This man Daniel . . . was found to have a keen mind (*same Hebrew word for excellent*) . . . and solve difficult problems. Call for Daniel . . ." (Dan. 5:12 NLT, *emphasis added*).

As it relates to this study on wealth, have you been using the "excellent spirit" God gave you to solve problems? How could you shift your thinking and actions to better tap into your creative power?

_____

_____

Like Daniel, the world is calling for you to solve difficult problems!

You have to be prepared for this calling. Consider the words Jesus shared in Luke 9:62 (NLT): "But Jesus told him, 'Anyone who puts a hand to the plow and then looks back is not fit for the Kingdom of God.'"

Jesus is not referring to being worthy or deserving; rather, He wants us to get fit to operate in His Kingdom.

How would you rate your "fitness level" to operate in God's Kingdom? Why?

_____

_____

_____

_____

Personal Application

What sphere of influence do you feel called to serve?

_____

_____

With God's help, what specific things do you want to do in that area?

_____

_____

_____

_____

It is time to get in shape!

Between You and God

Dear Heavenly Father, I know You have given me a powerful and precious gift—the ability to create wealth. Help me to see and use what You gave me. Help me to identify and remove any thoughts, beliefs, or actions that are in conflict with this gift, so I may use it to significantly serve others and glorify You.

Capture Your Learning

Please consider the following as you journal:

- ❏ What did you discover about your relationship with wealth and money that is worth noting?

- ❏ What aspect of this session stood out to you?

- ❏ What is God speaking to you regarding your assignment and getting "fit" for greater influence?

Corridor of the Experts

Get additional insights from Tim and other experts at

www.PowerToCreate.org

Notes from the Expert Videos:

_____

_____

_____

_____

_____

_____

_____

In our next session we are going to discover what God had in mind when He gave us the gift in Deuteronomy 8:18 . . .

Answers to the Companion Exercise for Video Session 1:
1. fruit
2. warning
3. create
4. finances
5. well-being
6. wealth and money
7. negative
8. drive
9. purpose
10. attracts

POWER TO CREATE
Unlock Greater Purpose, Relationships & Finances

*To truly understand wealth,
view it through the lens of
God's nature and personality.*

—Tim Redmond

Session 2

An Interview with the Creator

PowerKeys

❏ Discover what God had in mind when He gave you the gift described in Deuteronomy 8:18.

❏ Overcome the two key lies of scarcity to move to a mindset of abundance.

❏ Understand that resources and your capacity to create value are virtually unlimited.

Companion Exercise for Video Session 2

1. Creating wealth is intended to be a sacred, holy, _____ process.

2. This gift (the power to create wealth) is pregnant with purpose to help you fulfill your _____.

3. One key aspect of God's nature is _____.

4. Shortages are due to a lack of creativity and/or a _____ of leadership.

5. The kingdom of scarcity defines "economics" as the supply and demand on the _____ of resources.

6. The first lie of scarcity says, "There is not _____."

7. The second lie of scarcity says, "_____ am not enough."

8. God is calling you to a place of poverty . . . so you can bring His _____ to that place!

9. Applying _____ to a resource can make the resource virtually unlimited.

10. Deficiency is the _____ of creativity.

My Notes from Video Session 2:

My Notes from Video Session 2:

Personal Discovery

Imagine YOU are interviewing God, and you ask Him to explain to you what He had in mind when He gave you the power to create wealth.

What would He tell you?

_____

_____

Start with His Heart

When God gave you the gift described in Deuteronomy 8:18, He gave you a gift from His heart, a gift that reflects the nature of who He is.

This viewpoint may revolutionize the way you look at wealth and your role in creating it. If "the power to create wealth" reflects His heart, it is intended to be a sacred, holy, dignified process.

To understand the power of this gift, view it through the lens of His nature and essence. When people do not see wealth from God's perspective, corruption and self-centeredness tend to manifest. Today's news headlines prove this to be true!

When people do not see wealth from God's perspective, corruption and self-centeredness tend to manifest.

What words or feelings come to mind when you think about the nature of God?

Now take a moment to reflect on the words you wrote, and consider how strongly you believe each characteristic applies to you. Place a number from 1-10 next to each word you wrote above, with 1 being a word that you don't feel applies to you at all, and 10 being a word that strongly applies to you.

What words stand out to you? Why?

_____

_____

_____

There is one word I would like you to consider in describing God's personality. As you search the scriptures, you will find this one word permeates so much of His nature. What is the word?

Abundance.

". . . [His] pathways drip with abundance" (Psalm 65:11).

Whatever God creates, He creates with the capacity to be abundant. In other words, He builds within His creations more than what is necessary and usually equipms them with the capacity to reproduce and multiply.

> *Whatever God creates, He creates with the capacity to be abundant.*

If you consider whether God created the earth with abundance or deficiency, your answer may reveal how you look at everything in life.

Yet you may wonder, "If God created the earth with abundance, why are there are so many 'shortages' in the world?"

Do you believe these shortages are part of God's lack of planning or due to mankind's wrong thinking and poor stewardship? Why?

_____

_____

Because of shortages, people are full of anxiety, fear, and conflict. This is not God's design nor is it the way He wants you to respond.

Jesus told us, "Peace I leave with you, My peace I give to you; not as the world gives do I give to you. Let not your heart be troubled, neither let it be afraid" (John 14:27).

He actually bestowed on us the power to operate in His kingdom of abundance and possibility despite the shortages that may be around us. However, using this power requires seeing things with eyes of faith and looking beyond deficiencies that exist.

From What Kingdom Are You Operating?

There are two kingdoms on the earth: the Kingdom of God and the kingdom of darkness. Each kingdom takes on the nature of its king. Each kingdom also has its own economic system that reflects the personality of its king.

Each kingdom also has its own economic system that reflects the personality of its king.

Depending on which kingdom you follow and operate from, your entire outlook, mood, and motives are influenced. It determines what you think is possible . . . or impossible.

From what kingdom have you been operating? Before you answer, examine these two kingdoms.

The kingdom of darkness is the kingdom of scarcity.

Textbooks define *economics* as a study of the supply and demand based on the scarcity of resources. Please keep in mind that this definition is nothing more than an assumption or viewpoint that reflects the values of the kingdom that controls it.

Scarcity is a belief that the world is finite, a belief that says, "There is not enough and there will never be enough." In other words, there is only one pie, and if my piece of that grows bigger, then yours must shrink smaller.

A belief is simply an opinion of what we think is true. It is a viewpoint and an assumption and is not always based on truth.

What scarcity-based beliefs might you have in regard to your relationships, work, and finances?

_____

_____

_____

Why is it so important to move from scarcity to abundance when solving problems, serving others, and fulfilling your purpose?

_____

_____

_____

Many assumptions are wrapped up in the mindset of scarcity. I am suggesting that they are lies based on inaccurate observations of the world.

This curriculum covers two primary lies of scarcity.

Having a mindset of "not enough" affects how you see everything in your life.

The First Lie of Scarcity

Lie #1—There is not enough.

Scarcity is NOT just about money. Having a mindset of "not enough" affects how you see everything in your life. The voice of scarcity says, "There is not enough time, education, sleep, exercise, work, or influence. There are not enough trustworthy friends, days off, sales, or profits." The list is without end.

This lie is so pervasive, it dominates most people's day from the time they wake up until the time they fall asleep. It creates a chronic sense of inadequacy and anxiety because it works overtime to get people to think they never measure up and never have enough.

Most anxiety is based on a set of assumptions, not actual circumstances.

When your attention is on what is lacking and scarce in your life, then that becomes what you are about. Your focus drives you to strive and chase after what is missing. Those thoughts and fears grow from the attention you give them and can overtake your life!

Scarcity looks at the world as deficient rather than abundant. Seeing through this lens causes everything we think, say or do—especially in regards to money—to center around an endless effort to overcome the sense of lack and the fear of losing to others or being left out. On the other side of the coin, scarcity also breeds jealousy and covetousness.

How do you think the first lie of scarcity shows up in your life? Why?

Signs that Follow

In Mark 16:17, Jesus made a profound statement, "And these signs will follow those who believe. . . ."

He then spoke about many signs of the believer (vv. 17-18). In this passage, He unveiled what creates so many of the results in our lives. Here it is:

Signs will follow what you believe.

In other words, whatever you believe will produce signs. Signs are the recurring thoughts, feelings, actions, and results in your mind and life.

The beliefs that produce the signs are not what you "ought to believe" or "want to believe," but they are what you most deeply believe is true.

What "signs" are following your life in the areas of family and close relationships?

_____

_____

_____

_____

_____

_____

What "signs" are following your life in your work and finances?

_____

_____

_____

_____

_____

What "signs" are following your life in your dreams and desires?

_____

_____

_____

_____

_____

The Second Lie of Scarcity

Lie #2—I am not enough.

This lie can produce far more devastating results than the first lie of scarcity. A feeling of "I am not enough" is a sense of inadequacy that can be so deeply engrained that it invades all aspects of a person's life.

With this lie in operation, one feels he is not enough to overcome the challenge, to reconcile the relationship, or to create something beautiful from the ashes of disaster.

If you embrace this lie, you surrender and conform to the very world God has called you to creatively transform.

If you embrace this lie, you surrender and conform to the very world God has called you to creatively transform.

The lie that drove Adam and Eve to eat the fruit in the garden at the beginning of time was scarcity. The first couple thought, "What God gave me is not enough—and I am not enough. I need something more than what God has already given me."

When you forget who you really are, your whole approach to life is based on the ever-present sense of lack and inadequacy.

Yet God has created you to defy circumstances in the same way that Jesus did with the storms, water, and fish. He said, "Most assuredly, I say to you, he who believes in Me, the works that I do he will do also; and greater works than these he will do, because I go to My Father" (John 14:12).

Jesus wants to stretch the borders of your possibilities. As you read this, I hope this is your desire as well.

God has made you His masterpiece (Eph. 2:10 NLT). He has made you complete in Him (Col. 2:10). This is NOT referring to you AFTER you do this or become that—these are "right now" realities!

You were not made to conform to your outside world. You are equipped to transform it because of who you are on the inside.

Most Christians have no problem believing that God wants to use them to spread His love, compassion, peace, and wisdom. So why not also His abundance?

God is calling you to a place where poverty has been ruling, so you can bring His abundance to that place!

The challenge is agreeing with God and accepting what He is saying about you. Philemon 1:6 declares that the sharing of your faith would become more powerful by acknowledging every good thing which is in you in Christ Jesus.

When was the last time you acknowledged anything great about what is on the inside of you? Write down three powerful and positive things that are true about you based on this session.

1. _____

2. _____

3. _____

Break out of the contradictions and self-sabotaging thoughts and begin to agree with your original design; begin to agree with the gift God gave you in Deuteronomy 8:18!

Unlimited Nature of Wealth

Designed within that seed is the ability to infinitely multiply. You are like that seed.

Kingdom-based wealth has a very unusual quality to it. At its core, it is unlimited.

Wealth breeds wealth!

See this in the power of the seed. Imagine you are holding an apple seed in your hand. What do you see? Most will see just an apple seed.

However, some will look at the seed not as it is but as what it is capable of becoming. They may see an entire apple tree. Some may see packed into that little seed a vast apple orchard of hundreds of trees producing thousands of apples.

The power of that seed is unlimited!

A seed is like a "purpose packet" that when unleashed begins to rearrange the elements around it to a higher level of reality and a more valuable existence. Designed within that seed is the ability to infinitely multiply.

You are like that seed.

In a study of rich and poor nations, Mariano Grondona found that these two types of nations look at resources very differently.[1]

He observed that poor countries measure resources by what is in the ground or in their hand. Rich countries measure resources by the creativity applied to what is in the ground or in their hand.

Consider Japan after World War Two. It had (and still has) very limited natural resources, but it became an economic powerhouse. How? The people of Japan purchased resources from other countries, applied their creativity to the resources, and produced remarkable products.

In light of this perspective, how have you been measuring YOUR resources (money, talents, skills, assets, etc.)?

---

[1] *Culture Matters* by Lawrence Harrison and Samuel P. Huntington, chapter 4—"A Cultural Typology of Economic Development" by Mariano Grondona, Basic Books, copyright 2000.

What creative ideas are resident within you that are going to cause you to multiply what is in your hand? These do not have to be fully-formed ideas. Think freely—be sure not to limit your creativity at this stage.

1. _____

2. _____

3. _____

4. _____

5. _____

Remember: Deficiency is the shortage of creativity. A shortage of resources is not necessarily a hindrance to creating wealth.

Flipping Things Right-Side-Up

When you deliberately create to serve and give, you move from a limiting mindset of scarcity to a liberating mindset of abundance.

At the heart of the Kingdom of God is giving.

Giving is a lifestyle of instinctively seeing a need and meeting it. Creating to serve others is just as much an act of giving as putting money into an offering bucket (both are very important!).

When you deliberately create to serve and give, you move from a limiting mindset of scarcity to a liberating mindset of abundance.

The Variety Show

There is one aspect of God that is often overlooked or undervalued, but it is something bursting from His heart. This expression of God is a key element in understanding wealth and the gift He gave us. What am I referring to?

Variety.

God loves variety! Consider the differences among God's creation all around you—especially between the people with whom you are closest.

Another way of saying it is *infinite uniqueness.*

One of the Hebrew words for *money* literally means "the palm of your hands and the soles of your feet." It is with your hands you create something of value and with your feet you transport it to the people who need it.

Your hands—or "instruments of wealth"—are stamped with a mark of uniqueness from your Creator (like fingerprints). Each is as unique as your own ability to create wealth.

"God has given each of you a gift from his great variety of spiritual gifts. Use them well to serve one another" (1 Peter 4:10 NLT).

Back to Our Interview with the Creator

So what did You (God) have in mind when You gave us this gift?

Hear what He may have said . . .

"In the same way I blew a breath of greatness into Adam, I blew a unique breath into you . . . of abilities, gifts, assignments, and callings. I filled each of My children with a unique breath of creative power. It is power to create solutions and responses that demonstrate My nature and better connect you with one another.

"I filled Adam with a unique breath to enable him to bring into the earth the unique contributions he was designed to create. In the same way, at the beginning of your life, I breathed a unique breath of life into you to enable you to bring forth wealth and value into this world.

"I created you in My image. I created you to create. So when you see a problem, create a solution. When you see a difficulty, I want you to make a way. When you see lack, I have equipped you to bring abundance to that place."

Personal Application

What unique gifts do you believe God has given you?

_____

_____

_____

_____

_____

Based on these gifts, what simple actions might you take to create something of value for someone?

_____

_____

_____

_____

_____

Between You and God . . .

Dear Heavenly Father, I see now that You are excited about the unique gift You gave me to create wealth. Please show me clearly what this gift is and how I can immediately begin to develop and use it to serve others well. Help me remove any trace of scarcity from my thinking; and help me move into increasing levels of abundant thinking, living, and giving.

Capture Your Learning

Please consider the following as you journal:

❏ Think of all the aspects of God's nature and how each ties into the gift He gave you in Deuteronomy 8:18.

❏ Do you realize more deeply how unique is the gift He has given you?

❏ How do the lies of scarcity work to blind you from your power to create wealth?

❏ What became very clear to you during this session that you can apply practically to your life?

_____

_____

_____

_____

_____

_____

_____

_____

_____

_____

_____

Corridor of the Experts

Get additional insights from Tim and other experts at

www.PowerTo-Create.org

Notes from the Expert Videos:

_____

_____

_____

_____

_____

_____

_____

_____

In our next session we are going to unveil key details of the gift He imparted to each one of us!

Answers to the Companion Exercise for Video Session 2:
1. dignified
2. purpose
3. abundance
4. corruption
5. scarcity
6. enough
7. I
8. abundance
9. creativity
10. shortage

POWER TO CREATE
Unlock Greater Purpose, Relationships & Finances

True wealth is focused more on creating value to serve others than it is on accumulating possessions.

—Tim Redmond

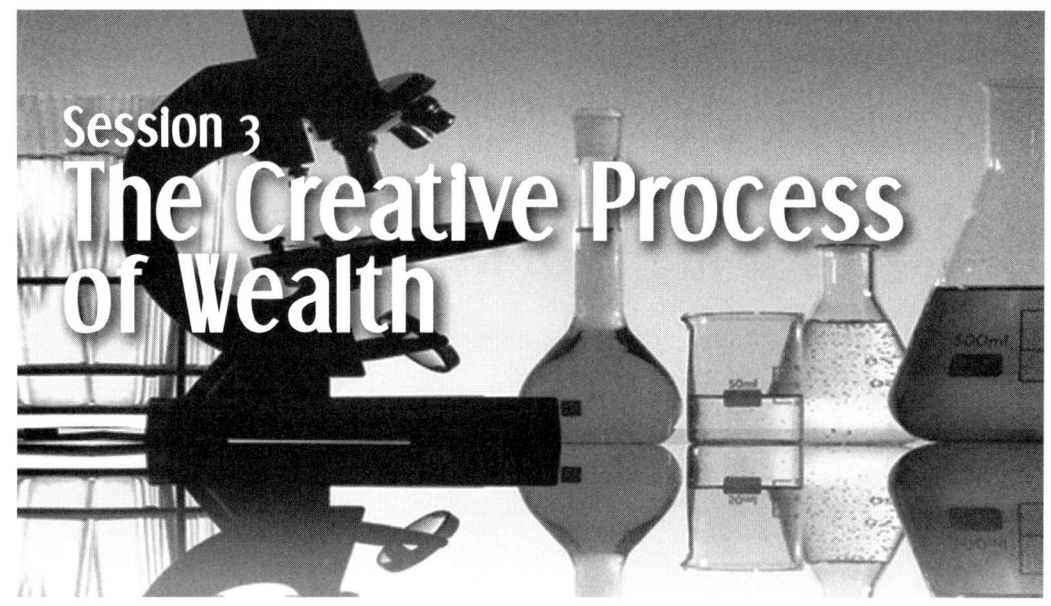

Session 3

The Creative Process of Wealth

PowerKeys . . .

❏ Bring your concept of wealth from a "far away" concept that seemingly affects only a few to something you can immediately get involved with right now.

❏ Redefine wealth from a Kingdom perspective—wealth is more about what flows FROM you rather than TO you.

❏ Mistakes, disappointments, and pain are the launching pad for great opportunities.

Companion Exercise for Video Session 3

1. The first action word in Bible is "_____". It sets the framework for the life God has designed for you to live.

2. From the Kingdom perspective, wealth is not something that comes to you, but flows _____ you.

3. Wealth is not as much the accumulation of goods as it is creating value to _____ other people.

4. A class at Harvard University concluded that happiness comes not by the accumulation of possessions but by the _____ of your heart!

5. What _____ can I solve right now?

6. Business is any _____ in which you create a product or service to help others.

7. Business is the most vivid demonstration of God's creative _____.

8. Things of value _____, things that lack value repel.

9. Wealth is mixing what is in your _____ with what is in your heart.

10. Many times, the place of greatest _____ becomes the launching pad for your opportunity.

My Notes from Video Session 3:

My Notes from Video Session 3:

Personal Discovery

How does God look at wealth? Is it something He is seeking after? Is He busy gathering and hoarding wealth?

The first verse in the Bible unveils the way God relates to wealth. Keep in mind that Genesis, especially the first chapter, is not just a history book but a pattern God wants us to follow.

The first action word in the Bible sets the framework for the way we are to look at life and reality. What is the word?

Created.

"In the beginning God created the heavens and the earth" (Gen. 1:1).

The nature of God is creative. He introduced Himself in the first verse of the Bible doing the thing He loves to do—create.

With God, wealth is not as much as what comes TO Him as flows FROM Him. Wealth is a creative process.

How does understanding God's perspective on wealth affect your perspective on wealth? Why is this so important?

You are created in the image of God. You are designed to operate like Him, to look at situations and challenges like He looks at them, and to interact with the world around you with confidence and faith like He does. Why?

". . . because as He is, so are we in this world" (1 John 4:17).

Say this out loud right now: "As God is, so am I in this world!"

Genesis 1:1 is a response for you to follow. In the beginning, God created. In the beginning of your day, prepare to "live your design." Start by creating towards rather than reacting against.

> In the beginning, God created. In the beginning of your day, prepare to "live your design." Start by creating towards rather than reacting against.

In the beginning of anything you do—whether solving a problem, nurturing a relationship, or doing a job, you are designed to create value in that situation.

Consider your approach towards your work. How would you evaluate your approach—creating towards or reacting against? Why?

_____

_____

_____

How about your approach towards your key relationships—are you creating towards or reacting against? Why?

_____

_____

_____

Some look at wealth as a far-away, unreachable concept reserved only for a few fortunate people. Yet God has given YOU the power to create wealth. He has equipped you with the capacity to create it NOW!

Pursue Purpose or Possessions?

With the focus on consumerism, image, and reputation, many are side-tracked pursuing results instead of their purpose. It has become a rat race towards the accumulation of possessions. In fact, since World War II in the US and many other countries, people have doubled the "stuff" they own.

With the focus on consumerism, image, and reputation, many are side-tracked pursuing results instead of their purpose.

Despite this huge increase in possessions, the rate of depression over the same period has increased by 300 percent. Some have even estimated depression has increased 1000 percent! Having stuff is not wrong but it is definitely not the answer.

Think about your own personal wealth history. Have your times of greatest joy, fulfillment, and creativity always occurred during times when your bank account has been the biggest? Write down your thoughts and memories.

One of the most popular classes at Harvard University is called Positive Psychology. It is a study of what causes happiness. Interestingly, they found happiness comes not by the accumulation of possessions but by the contribution of the heart!

Looking beyond ourselves and our needs in order to help others is a huge step in curing depression.

Wealth is creating value to serve others.

Creating wealth has more to do with purpose than possessions. Wealth in its truest form is more focused on creating value to serve others than it is on accumulating possessions or serving self.

This is the core definition of wealth from the perspective of God's Kingdom:

Wealth is creating value to serve others.

What you pursue defines you. In God's Kingdom, wealth is NOT focused on pursuing money and possessions; rather, it is focused on serving others. It is seeing people's needs and meeting them.

Yes, money and possessions are indeed part of the "all these things will be added to you" that Jesus specified when He told us to seek first the Kingdom of God—the Kingdom that is focused on serving others. (See Matt. 6:33.)

We are created to create. Creating is a high form of giving. This kind of giving is focused on making valuable, meaningful, practical "gifts" (products and services) to serve others. Creating and providing value is your purpose in action. That is why Jesus said it is more blessed to give than to receive!

You can create value in an infinite number of ways. Designing buildings, teaching students, making music, sweeping floors, raising children, generating ideas, taking action, developing products and services . . . even a hug and a timely word of encouragement are forms of creating value.

We must renew our minds to the truth about wealth and not make it a mysterious, inaccessible concept. Wealth is simply creating value to serve others in meaningful ways.

What are some of the ways you can create value to serve others at home, work, and church this week?

Opportunities to meet the needs of others are all around you. What are some new ways you can do this right now with the resources you have?

_____

_____

_____

Creating value is the focal point of the wealth process. If you are not creating, you are not fulfilling your purpose.

Minding Your Business

I define "business" in much the same way I define wealth: business is simply creating value (a product or service) to serve others. That means all of us are in some type of business, whether we work in a formal business or not. God is giving us the power to run our "business" in increasingly valuable ways.

Business is the most vivid demonstration of God's creative compassion.

We are to join Jesus in being about our Father's business. (See Luke 2:49.)

Based on your resources, relationships, dreams, ideas, and unique gifts you have been given, what "business" are you in?

_____

_____

_____

In God's economic system, He designed you to meet the needs and wants of others in compelling and memorable ways. It is an expression of His creative compassion!

The more you help others, the happier and more satisfied you become. Plus, the better you get at it, the more money and possessions you will attract in and through your life. These are just some of the by-products of the wealth process.

Attract or Repel?

If wealth is creating value to serve others, the challenge we face is increasing our value and expanding our "serve." God gave you the ability to create increasing levels of value to serve expanding numbers of people.

Value attracts, the lack value repels.

Value attracts, the lack of value repels.

What level of value are you creating? Is it valuable enough that someone would want to pay you or exchange value with you?

The key focus is increasing the level of value you produce.

After one seminar I conducted, a man wanted to talk to me. With his face filled with anxiety, he asked, "What you are saying doesn't work! I create value to serve others, but I am always struggling financially."

I could see his frustration and my heart opened up to him. After asking him a few questions, I explained that creating value is an ongoing development process in which you keep improving your skills.

As you look at your personal history of wealth and value creation, how have you seen this to be true?

How are you actively working on your skills to increase the value you produce?

Value is perceived in the eyes of the beholder. The way you carry and project yourself sometimes has as much to do with how your value is measured as the work you actually do.

The way you carry and project yourself sometimes has as much to do with how your value is measured as the work you actually do.

The man who approached me with his concern did not look like he put much value in the way he presented himself. I am not referring to how expensive his clothes were but rather how well he had groomed and carried himself.

How would you evaluate the way you carry yourself—your posture, tone, appearance, confidence, etc.? Are you projecting value or not?

_____

_____

_____

What is one practical thing you can do immediately to improve this?

_____

_____

_____

Although you do not want to be controlled by the opinions of others, you want them to correctly perceive you as having something valuable to contribute. God does look at the heart, but people are influenced by your appearance. (See 1 Sam. 16:7.)

Do you think others see what you are doing or creating as valuable? Why?

_____

_____

_____

If it does not appear that they are right now, don't lose heart and don't give up! Stay in the game. Keep working intimately with the Giver of your gift to help you serve others in increasingly significant ways.

Show Me the Money!

Do you need money to create wealth? This is a BIG question with which many struggle.

Money is helpful, but is it absolutely necessary to begin the wealth creation process? The way you answer this question determines how limited or liberated you feel about acting on the idea or project you want to pursue.

Do you have an idea you have not acted on yet? Is one of the reasons "not enough money"?

When you think of wealth as a creative process, money is the lowest form of wealth. It is a temporary holding place to exchange true wealth such as food, buildings, or influence.

Money is a bad leader but a great follower. Remember . . . money follows value.

Money is a bad leader but a great follower. Remember . . . money follows value.

Consider Bill Gates, the founder of Microsoft. He began learning how to write computer programs while in secondary school. Did he have to have money to get started? No. He used the school's computers to develop his skills and to increase the value he could produce. He eventually became good enough at programming that people began to pay him for the software he wrote. With the development of his skills over time, billions of dollars followed the value he and his company produced.

If money were not an obstacle, what ideas, journeys, or activities would you like to act upon or accomplish?

1. _____

2. _____

3. _____

What actions can you begin to take now towards one of the items on your list above?

_____

_____

_____

What Is In Your Hand?

Wealth is mixing what is in your hand with what is in your heart.

What is "in your hand" includes skills, experiences, education, relationships, and assets.

Wealth is mixing what is in your hand with what is in your heart.

It can even include things you might consider a liability. In God's Kingdom, there is never a wound that is wasted or a hurt that can't be helpful.

Even if the only thing you have in your hand is the pain of a divorce or financial devastation, these can be the raw ingredients to create value that helps others. Many people who have suffered horribly in these areas are now actively helping others walk through the very pain they struggled through.

Even if the only thing you have in your hand is the pain of a divorce or financial devastation, these can be the raw ingredients to create value that helps others.

So many have the tendency to discount or despise what is in their hand and life, especially if it has pain and shame attached to it. Know that as you love and pursue God, He creatively orchestrates all things to work together for your good. (See Rom. 8:28.)

What is in your hand? (skills, experiences, victories, setbacks, education, relationships, and assets)

_____

_____

_____

_____

_____

Instead of looking at what is in your hand as something you despise, look at it as an essential raw material that will accelerate your capacity to create higher levels of value.

What Is In Your Heart?

Your heart is where the Creator of the universe lives! I am referring to the One who measured the universe with the span of His hand, multiplied the fish and loaves, parted and calmed the sea, walked on water, and turned an unproductive fishing enterprise into one that could hardly contain the increase in business!

Your heart is where the eternal, life-giving Word resides. "Your word I have hidden in my heart, that I might not sin against You" (Ps. 119:11).

The One who was not intimidated with the chaos, but instead hovered over and brought order to it resides in your heart—the Holy Spirit. He is a creative genius that is committed to be your Helper, Comforter, Teacher, Mentor, and Guide. He is personally interested in leading you to your wealthy place. (See Ps. 66:12 KJV.)

Within your heart, you can imagine anything you choose—even if it is completely opposite of what you see around you. God doesn't just speak to you in a language you can hear; He speaks to you in a language you can see.

As God begins to paint a picture of your calling and amazing future, you can nurture that vision and dream in your heart.

God doesn't just speak to you in a language you can hear; He speaks to you in a language you can see.

What dreams and ideas do you SEE in your heart today?

When you combine what is in your heart and in your hand with faith and confidence, you are operating a value-creation manufacturing plant!

Because of disappointments, pains, and insecurities, many have withdrawn their heart from the game. They stand safely on the sidelines watching instead of participating . . . and are miserable doing so!

Get your heart fully involved! Give yourself permission to get back on the field and play full

When you combine what is in your heart and in your hand with faith and confidence, you are operating a value-creation manufacturing plant!

out. That is the way your Creator designed you to operate, and He is your biggest fan and most enthusiastic cheerleader!

Any Place, Any Culture, Any Time

Again, wealth is creating value to serve others. This means wealth can be created anywhere, in any economic climate, in any culture, at any time.

However little or much you have in your hand, you can begin to create today.

Initially, you do not even have to know how; you just need to know that you can. The "how" will come as you give your heart permission to take action in creating ideas, products, and services to help others.

Frustrations, negative circumstances, and big problems are gift-wrapped wealth-creation opportunities.

God specializes in utilizing anything and every-thing in your life—the good, the bad, and especially the ugly.

Frustrations, negative circumstances, and big problems are gift-wrapped wealth-creation opportunities.

Mistakes and failures are key ingredients that God adds to the wealth-making recipe. These can actually enable you to effec-tively and significantly meet the needs of the people you are called to help.

Maneuver around the Roadblocks Ahead

Be aware, however; many have a tendency not to forgive themselves and others for their negative experiences. When you don't forgive, you stop your creative flow and shut down the gift God has imparted to you.

Forgiveness releases your wealth-creation abilities. Whom in your life (including yourself!) do you need to forgive, and how can you express your forgiveness?

Even your handicaps—both real and perceived—can be used to help you fulfill your purpose and touch the lives of people.

Handicaps can be a place of great pain in one's life; yet the place of greatest pain can become a launching pad for your opportunity.

Towards the end of Video Session 3, I shared my personal struggle with a handicap. Not only did I overcome it, but it became the focal point for what I am doing now (speaking and training leaders internationally)!

Today God is calling you to look differently at your challenges—whether they are due to mistakes, betrayals, disappointments, or handicaps. Your place of pain can become your place of opportunity.

Personal Application

What mistakes, disappointments, insecurities, or handicaps have defined your life and influenced where you are today?

How have you turned these around to become an avenue for you to create value to serve others? (And how can you do this right now?)

Between You and God . . .

Dear Heavenly Father, thank You for this amazing gift You have given me—the power to create wealth. I realize it has more to do with creating value to serve others than obtaining things to serve me. Lord, help me look at everything in my life—even my mistakes, betrayals of others, and handicaps—as the raw material to create significant and unique value to meet the needs of individuals and groups. Help me increase the value I produce, and expand my reach to help even more people. I thank You now for this and give You the credit and honor for what You and I will create together!

Capture Your Learning

Please consider the following as you journal:

❑ Think of how your definition of wealth and the gift God gave you in Deuteronomy 8:18 is expanding and becoming clearer.

❑ What skills and experiences have you disregarded or discounted in the past that can help you serve others better now?

❑ What became very clear to you during this session that you can apply practically to your life?

❑ What is God now giving you permission to do?

_____

_____

_____

_____

_____

_____

_____

_____

Corridor of the Experts

Get additional insights from Tim and other experts at

www.PowerToCreate.org

Notes from the Expert Videos:

_____

_____

_____

_____

_____

_____

_____

In our next session, we are going to further define wealth in ways you can immediately implement in your life.

Answers to the Companion Exercise for Video Session 3:

1. created
2. from
3. serve
4. contribution
5. opportunities
6. activity
7. compassion
8. attract
9. hand
10. pain

POWER TO CREATE
Unlock Greater Purpose, Relationships & Finances

The key to success is not avoiding the problem but learning to be creative in the problem.

—Tim Redmond

Session 4
Create or React?

PowerKeys . . .

❏ Define wealth in a way that liberates you to begin creating it immediately.

❏ Discover how to move from a reactive, victimized mindset to a creative, confident mindset.

❏ Learn how to have a proper relationship with problems and hardships so that they bring joy and abundance to you and others.

Companion Exercise for Video Session 4

1. With the *Power to Create* mindset, you don't have to _____ for money or resources to come to you before you begin creating.

2. Wealth is a _____ (so is poverty).

3. Wealth creates, poverty _____.

4. Are you going to _____ to situations, or are you going to begin to create in situations to transform them?

5. The secret is to _____ yourself beyond the challenge you are facing.

6. Abundance-minded people _____ for problems!

7. *Power to Create* gives you the ability to adapt and _____ even in the harshest of environments.

8. Don't run away from the chaos; rather _____ over it!

9. When opportunities first appear, they don't always look _____.

10. Don't _____ your talent and your opportunity.

My Notes from Video Session 4:

My Notes from Video Session 4:

Personal Discovery

Creating value to serve others describes your purpose. It is working with God and the gift He has given you to enrich the lives of others.

As covered in the previous session, you do not have to wait for money or resources to come to you first. Begin to create with whatever is in your hand (resources) and heart (creative faith).

Are you currently facing a challenge? Is it related to your family, a relationship, work, or finances?

Briefly write down the challenge that immediately came to mind.

_____

_____

_____

_____

As you were writing, what emotions did you feel?

_____

_____

_____

Wealth Further Defined

Wealth as explained previously is creating value to serve others, but there is another key definition of Kingdom-based wealth.

Wealth is a response. It is created by how you respond to situations and the people in them.

> *Wealth is a response. It is created by how you respond to situations and the people in them.*

Poverty is also a response.

Wealth is a creative response; poverty is a reactive response.

Based on this definition and what you wrote in the previous section, how would you assess YOUR response to your current situation?

_____

_____

_____

In this session's video, I explained the two ways I responded to the various challenges regarding my four-unit apartment building. My initial response was reactive. Realizing what I was doing, I changed my approach. However, when more bad news came, I immediately reverted back to a reactive, victimized response.

When I finally committed whole-heartedly to take whatever action was necessary AND began to move relentlessly towards resolving the challenge, the solution came.

We Need Help

Success is not for the weak at heart. To move from reacting to creating requires strength and a firm decision. Success is not for the weak at heart.

That is why Paul prayed that you would be strengthened by God's Spirit in your inward man. "For this reason I bow my knees to the Father of our Lord Jesus Christ, from whom the whole family in heaven and earth is named, that He would grant you, according to the riches of His glory, to be strengthened with might through His Spirit in the inner man" (Eph. 3:14-16).

Responding poorly in your relationships, to issues at work, and to changes in the world around you will create some form of poverty in your life.

How would you evaluate the way you are responding at home, work, and in your key relationships?

_____

_____

_____

What is one way you can respond that would make a big difference for you and the people with whom you interact?

_____

_____

_____

Wealth Creates, Poverty Reacts

To live reactively is to play the role of a victim. All of us have suffered injustice or have been hurt by those we love and trust. The pain from these situations runs deep, often to the point where we are not even conscious of our patterns of response.

Many live under the shadow of a negative experience and allow it to control them. It becomes the excuse they use for not growing, taking risks, and tapping their creative potential. Reliance upon these excuses creates a victim mentality.

Victims are paralyzed by thinking they do not have any choices. They feel stuck and controlled by something outside of themselves, like the economy, a mean boss, a hurtful parent, or the betrayal of a trusted friend.

When you believe a lie, you give power to that lie to begin to control you.

Feeling stuck is an illusion. It is a lie. When you believe a lie, you give power to that lie to begin to control you.

Without minimizing your specific experiences or the hurt they caused, you still have a choice about how you are going to respond.

God has given you the power to choose! "I have set before you life and death, blessing and cursing; therefore choose life . . ." (Deut. 30:19). "You are of God, little children, and have overcome them, because He who is in you is greater than he who is in the world" (1 John 4:4).

A victim responds by sitting down, doing nothing, and hoping the situation will eventually turn for the better. You are more than that! It is time to stand up and remind that situation who the boss is.

In what situations have you been responding like a victim?

1. _____

2. _____

3. _____

With each of these challenges, what is one thing you can do to move from being victimized by it to creating in the midst of the challenge and transforming it?

1. _____

   _____

2. _____

   _____

3. _____

   _____

The key to responding in a creative way is this: do not avoid the problem, but instead learn to be creative in the problem.

Do you remember Sir Edmund Hillary's first experience climbing Mt. Everest? After failing to reach the summit, he turned to the picture of the mountain and declared, "You have grown as big as you will ever be; but I am still growing and I am going to conquer you!" The next year, he became the first person to reach the peak of the world's tallest mountain.

Grow yourself beyond the challenge you are facing.

Instead of being controlled by the outside world, combine your gift with God's unlimited creativity. You are empowered to create abundance where there appears to be lack.

Look for and Love Problems!

Think of the most successful companies in the world. They are masters at solving problems and providing attractive solutions. Most of these companies have countered a downturn in their business by looking for more problems to solve!

They have a different relationship with challenges. For most, problems are bad and to be avoided. When they see one, they run the other way. This is not how successful people think.

Most of these companies have countered a downturn in their business by looking for more problems to solve!

Abundance-minded people look for problems to solve! When they find one, they get excited because it represents an opportunity to serve others and create wealth!

Think of a particular negative situation or unresolved issue. Describe your relationship with it (how you feel, your energy and confidence levels, etc.)

Use everything—good and bad—as an opportunity for personal growth. Turn every circumstance into an opportunity to develop wisdom and skills.

Turn every circumstance into an opportunity to develop wisdom and skills.

As you adapt this approach, you will find your ability to create compelling solutions will continue to rise even in difficult times.

Our key verse, Deuteronomy 8:18, states that God gives us the power to create wealth.

Strong's Concordance denotes that the word *power* is related to a large lizard or chameleon. Just as He has given a lizard the ability to adapt and thrive even in the harshest of environments, God is giving you the power and ability to produce regardless of your situation!

How God Responds to a Mess

Your God-given gift to create value is attracted to messes and chaos.

Would you believe that your God-given gift to create value is attracted to messes and chaos?

God showed up in the first verse of the Bible as a Creator. It only took Him one verse to run into a mess. Genesis 1:2 says that the earth was dark and chaotic.

God's response in this verse is the example we are to follow. He did not run away from the mess. Instead, He hovered over, spoke life, and brought order to it. This is wealth creation in action!

How did Jesus respond to the messes and shortages when He ran into them? (At a wedding, after a bad night of fishing, during tax time, and even with the lack of innocent blood needed for the ultimate sacrifice.)

_____

_____

_____

Hear what God may be saying to you right now. "Do you see the way I responded to the chaos? I want you to respond the same way to the chaos in your life! I have equipped you to bring order, value, and beauty to that situation. Do not run away from it—hover over and speak life to it!"

So how are you responding to the challenges in your life?

Revisit the challenge you wrote down during the video session or earlier in this Workbook chapter. How did you feel about the challenge when you wrote it down—reactive or creative? Why?

Based on what you are learning in this session, how can you respond creatively to this challenge?

Do Joy and Trouble Mix?

James 1:2 instructs us how to have a proper relationship with challenges and hardships: respond by counting it ALL joy when you experience them. The *New Living Translation* version says it well, "Dear brothers and sisters, when troubles come your way, consider it an opportunity for great joy."

What kind of odd response is that? "Troubles" and "great joy" do not seem a likely match. Why would anyone want to respond with joy to a difficult situation?

The verse that follows holds the answer. You can count it all joy when you know what is actually going on behind the scenes—namely that your faith is on trial.

This process is helping you to work with and rely on God in greater ways, causing your creative capacity—your ability to create something valuable out of the difficulty—to grow and become more fruitful. Your faith is being tempered like a special metal alloy made to perform with excellence in even the harshest of environments.

When you stand strong and endure (patience) in that testing time, your maturity accelerates and your value-creating capacity expands to a point where you lack nothing.

The Joy of Dreaming

The root word for *dreaming* means "to joy." How would you respond if all of your dreams were fulfilled in spectacular ways? What overflowing emotion would bubble up in a dramatic way? Joy!

In the hectic pace of life, it seems there is an endless supply of troubles. When the battle seems relentless, we may forget who we are and allow the challenges to rob us of our joy. If that happens, our dreams are in danger of being stolen.

Based on this understanding of the relationship between challenges, joy, and dreams, how have your joy and dreams been affected?

_____

_____

_____

Learning to respond creatively instead of reactively is a strategy to protect and nurture your dreams.

Don't discard or diminish your dreams in the middle of a battle. Take joy knowing there is an amazing development process at work within you even now as you read.

God birthed a dream within you. Tap into the Kingdom of God—the kingdom of righteousness, peace, and joy. (See Rom. 14:17.) As you confidently and creatively embrace the hardships as opportunities to strengthen your faith, it will stimulate joy within your heart and move you towards your dreams.

God specializes in resurrecting dreams . . . especially yours!

Learning to respond creatively instead of reactively is a strategy to protect and nurture your dreams.

More than Meets the Eye

God loves messes. More accurately, He loves to hover over and bring order to messes. The opportunities that come to us frequently look unattractive, especially in the beginning.

Therefore it is critical to have a proper relationship with the circumstances we face. Without it, we might walk away from the very opportunities God is presenting to us!

It is critical to have a proper relationship with the circumstances we face. Without it, we might walk away from the very opportunities God is presenting to us!

Think about how the "Pancake Lady" I described in the Video Session initially responded to the opportunity that was given to her. She could not see past the pain and lack in her life to creatively apply herself to meet a need in her community. It blinded her of her potential and caused her to despise her talent and opportunity.

But as she picked herself up and began to take action making pancakes, she put her wealth-creation gears into motion. She began to develop skills and gained insights to help her serve more and more people.

Her little steps (which seemed insignificant) led to big steps that changed her family, church, and city!

If she could change her future and entire city with pancakes, what can God do through you?

Instead of reacting or running away from the hardships, begin to create towards them! What a great wealth habit to form!

Personal Application

What are your dreams? If you do not know exactly, that is alright. You can gain some clarity by answering these questions:

❏ What are some things you like to do?

❏ Where would you like to go?

❏ What group of people would you like to help and how would you help them?

❏ What kinds of creative work brings you joy?

❏ What positive desires have stayed with you for many years?

What challenges seem opposed to your dreams? How might you bring creative faith to them?

_____

_____

_____

How can you further prepare yourself to accomplish your dreams?

_____

_____

_____

Between You and God . . .

Dear Heavenly Father, You are the great Creator. I am amazed at Your ability to create practical and beautiful things out of a mess! You have empowered me to follow in Your footsteps. Help me to have the right relationship with the challenges in my life, so I can embrace them with great joy. Thank You for empowering me to create towards them instead of reacting against them. Work in and through me now that I may confidently and creatively manage hardships and demonstrate Your Kingdom for Your glory and praise.

Capture Your Learning

Please consider the following as you journal:

❏ Think about how you have changed your perspective on the challenge(s) you wrote down.

❏ What is God calling you to overcome, and what is He saying to you about it?

❏ What became very clear to you during this session that you can apply practically to your life?

_____

_____

_____

_____

_____

_____

_____

_____

_____

_____

_____

_____

_____

_____

_____

_____

Corridor of the Experts

Get additional insights from Tim and other experts at
www.PowerToCreate.org

Notes from the Expert Videos:

_____

_____

_____

_____

_____

_____

_____

In our next session, we are going to tap into the power of "Wow!" It will generate what the currency of the Kingdom of God is all about.

Answers to the Companion Exercise for Video Session 4

1. wait
2. response
3. reacts
4. conform
5. grow
6. look
7. thrive
8. hover
9. attractive
10. despise

POWER TO CREATE

Unlock Greater Purpose, Relationships & Finances

*The currency of the world is money;
the currency of the Kingdom
is connection.*

—Tim Redmond

Session 5
Relationships That Produce "Wow!"

PowerKeys . . .

- ❏ Discover why wealth has more to do with discovering and living your purpose than it does generating money.

- ❏ Everything in the Kingdom of God revolves around building and nurturing relationships.

- ❏ God desires to work intimately and creatively with you to make a significant impact on others.

Companion Exercise for Video Session 5

1. Purpose #1: Equip you to fulfill your _____ more effectively.

2. Purpose #2: For your personal _____.

3. Purpose #3: Draw you to walk and work more _____ with Him.

4. The currency of the world is money; the currency of the Kingdom is _____.

5. A call to create wealth is a call to _____ intimacy with Him.

6. One of the Hebrew words for *businessman* means "man of _____."

7. The Holy Spirit wants to work intimately with you to expand your _____ of possibility.

8. God wants to be your_____ on the journey of success.

9. The focus of God and His Kingdom is _____.

10. Kingdom-focused wealth is co-creating with God to _____ others.

My Notes from Video Session 5:

My Notes from Video Session 5:

Personal Discovery

God is a God of purpose. He does things on purpose, for a purpose.

"Indeed I have spoken it; I will also bring it to pass. I have purposed it; I will also do it" (Is. 46:11). "Having made known to us the mystery of His will, according to His good pleasure which He purposed in Himself" (Eph. 1:9). Every gift God gives us is pregnant with purpose to help us fulfill our purpose. There are three purposes wrapped up in the gifts He gives us—especially the gift described in Deuteronomy 8:18.

> *Every gift God gives us is pregnant with purpose to help us fulfill our purpose.*

Purpose #1 — God gave you the power to create wealth to equip you to fulfill your purpose and assignment more effectively.

How would you describe your purpose in one word or a short phrase? Write down whatever comes to mind, even if you list several items:

_____

_____

_____

_____

An assignment can be looked at from two perspectives. First, it refers to your grand, lifetime assignment. Second, it refers to what you are doing now, which may not look anything like your ultimate purpose.

What comes to mind when you think of your grand, lifetime assignment?

_____

_____

_____

_____

At times, it may be a challenge to connect your current task to your lifetime assignment, and that is OK. What are the various things you are involved in right now?

_____

_____

_____

"Always be a student" is a motto commonly used by successful people. How does your education (both past formal classroom and present self-study) tie into your lifetime assignment?

_____

_____

_____

How does your paid and volunteer work connect with your lifetime assignment?

_____

_____

_____

How could your recreation and hobbies relate to your lifetime assignment?

_____

_____

_____

_____

Purpose #2 — God gave you the power to create for your personal enjoyment.

How did that statement strike you when you first read it? Do you fully believe it? Why?

_____

_____

If you are a parent, think of a time you gave your children a gift. Do you remember the joy that welled up within you as you saw them using and enjoying it? Your Heavenly Father feels the same way about the gifts He gives you.

When you are busy creating and meeting the needs of others with the gift He gave you, you are happy, God is happy, and the people you serve are happy! There is joy for everyone!

Give yourself permission to enjoy—without apology or shame—the rewards that come to you for using your gift to serve others well. As you meet the needs of others, money, possessions, influence, and promotion will be added to you. Enjoy and share them with a thankful heart!

Paul instructed Timothy in a similar way. "Teach those who are rich in this world not to be proud and not to trust in their money, which is so unreliable. Their trust should be in God, who richly gives us all we need for our enjoyment" (1 Timothy 6:17 NLT).

God wants you to enjoy what He gives you!

Purpose #3—God gave you this gift, so you would walk and work more intimately with Him.

That is the focal point of this session. God is very invested and involved with this gift operating in your life. Just as I give a certain Christmas gift to my wife that says, "I come with this gift and will give you my attention and emotional support for an entire day of shopping" (yes, this is difficult to write!), God comes with the gift He has given you.

As you've begun to apply your gift over the past few weeks, have you felt His presence when you are creating value? Explain.

_____

_____

_____

_____

A call to create wealth is a call to intense intimacy with the Creator.

The following statement is one of the most important aspects of wealth creation: A call to create wealth is a call to intense intimacy with the Creator.

What does this statement mean to you?

_____

_____

_____

_____

As Paul warned his close friend and son in the faith, a lack of awareness of this truth has caused the downfall of many. "But if it's only money these leaders are after, they'll self-destruct in no time. Lust for money brings trouble and nothing but trouble. Going down that path, some lose their footing in the faith completely and live to regret it bitterly ever after" (1 Tim. 6:9-10 MSG).

Seek first God and His Kingdom to avoid being entangled or controlled by the things so many people pursue.

Called to a Place of Poverty?

I stated in this video session, "God is calling you to a place of poverty, so you can bring His abundance to that place." What does this statement mean to you?

_____

_____

_____

_____

How can you apply this statement practically in your work or family environment?

What is the poverty?	Where is it showing up?	What solution will you bring to that place to create abundance?

In giving you the power to create, God is excited to demonstrate His abundant nature with and through you, especially in difficult places. Do not run away from challenges; rather, hover over them and create!

Worship while You Work

One of the Hebrew words for *work* means "to fulfill your purpose."

From God's perspective, work is a sacred, dignified process in which you can worship Him by the quality of your output.

From God's perspective, work is a sacred, dignified process in which you can worship Him by the quality of your output. What a thought—your work can be a place where you worship God!

A closer look at 1 Peter 2:9 reinforces this truth. "But you are a chosen generation, a royal priesthood, a holy nation, His own special people. . . ." Why?

The rest of the verse in the *Amplified Bible* explains it well. "That you may . . . display the virtues and perfections of Him Who called you out of darkness into His marvelous light."

Demonstrating the virtues God has given you is a form of worship. You demonstrate His virtues wherever you are—especially doing your work, creating value, and fulfilling your purpose!

Do you feel that your work is a place where you fulfill your purpose?

_____

_____

_____

Even if the work you currently do is not what you are going to do for the rest of your life, what adjustments can you make in your thinking to make it a place where you fulfill your purpose?

_____

_____

_____

Your Faith—God's Pleasure

Each one of us is in business in some form. God is pleased when you put your heart into the business of creating and serving others regardless of what work it is. Why is this true?

You may not know how the people you serve will respond to your work; every action is a step of faith.

In the Hebrew language, one of the words for *businessperson* literally means "person of faith." "But without faith it is impossible to please Him, for he who comes to God must believe that He is, and that He is a rewarder of those who diligently seek Him" (Heb. 11:6).

God laughs with delight and pleasure as He sees you walking by faith in your work.

Write down two experiences from your "business." Note one example where your efforts to create value were not received well and one where your creativity was celebrated.

_____

_____

_____

_____

Based on what we are learning in this session, what is your perspective and takeaway from these experiences?

_____

_____

_____

Intimate Involvement

My father, Dr. William Redmond, was a chemical engineer. He struggled for several years trying to decide if ministry or engineering was where God wanted him to work. He did not realize at that time that his vocation *was* his ministry.

God loves Monday morning as much as Sunday morning!

Finally, when praying one morning, my father heard Jesus tell him, "I (Jesus) love to be a chemical engineer, and I love to be one through Bill Redmond!" In the same way, God loves work and He loves to do it with and through you! That is why God loves Monday morning as much as Sunday morning!

What does working intimately with God look like?

A verse in Psalms begins to reveal this concept. "The secret of the Lord is with those who fear Him, and He will show them His covenant" (Ps. 25:14). You do not yell a secret across the room. A secret is a close, intimate communication between those who trust one another.

To work more intimately with God means to grow in your understanding of who He is and how He works with you to bring you to levels of extraordinary creativity and performance.

The Holy Spirit will introduce ideas, concepts, and strategies that will help you expand your borders of possibility.

The Holy Spirit will introduce ideas, concepts, and strategies that will help you expand your borders of possibility. He will cause you to work more effectively or select the solution that will have the biggest impact for the lowest cost.

Jesus said that all things are possible to the one who believes. (See Mark 9:23.) There is a field of possibility where people bring things into reality whose time is come, including highly profitable inventions, solutions, approaches, and market opportunities.

The key is learning to listen to and work intimately with the Holy Spirit. When your heart is focused on creating to serve others, you can expect God to inspire you! He is very interested in this creative process and will teach you all the things you need to know.

People Who Change the World

Consider industry-shaping entrepreneurs like Steve Jobs of Apple Computers, Bill Gates of Microsoft, and Sam Walton of Wal-Mart. They had a huge capacity to sense emerging opportunities and began to act in harmony with them.

God wants to be your personal guide, and He is jealous for your attention. He wants to be your number-one Mentor, especially on your journey of creating value and solving difficult problems.

God wants to be your number-one Mentor, especially on your journey of creating value and solving difficult problems.

What God-inspired ideas are flowing in your mind? (Please note—these are not necessarily religious or church-related activities; rather, they are ideas to help and serve people better.)

What possibilities might you be ignoring? (These might be those "crazy" or "too-big" ideas you have been hiding deep inside.)

What little steps can you begin towards one of these ideas now?

_____

_____

_____

It's All about Relationships!

The gift God gave you, and the intimacy with which He wants to work with you, will help you build intimate relationship with others. Remember, the currency of the world is money; the currency of the Kingdom is connections.

I recently had a millionaire businessman friend challenge me with a question: "Why do you emphasize wealth so much? Isn't the focus of the Kingdom all about relationships?"

I agreed with him wholeheartedly. Then I asked him, "How do you create and strengthen relationships? How would your wife respond if you never created value for her like helping around the house and giving her presents, hugs, and loving words?"

> When you are not providing value into a relationship, you weaken it.

Relationships are nurtured by investing into them. When you bring value into a relationship, it will grow. When you are not providing value into a relationship, you weaken it.

God is giving you the power to start and nurture relationships by helping you create value to bring into them. That is what this gift is all about—building healthy, long-lasting relationships!

With whom are your key relationships? How can you create value to invest further into those relationships?

In Whom Are You Going to Invest?	How Are You Going to Create Value for This Person?

The Collective Force of an Army

The Hebrew word for *wealth* in Deuteronomy 8:18 is defined as a "collective force for a common purpose." The same Hebrew word is used for *army* and *band of soldiers* in other Bible passages. It denotes a community of people exchanging value with each other.

Wealth comes by increasing the quality and quantity of your transactions with others. The more people cooperate, interact, and exchange products and services with each other, the more wealth is created in a community.

Wealth comes by increasing the quality and quantity of your transactions with others.

The opposite is also true. The more mistrust, strife, and lack of connecting there is, the more a community will suffer economically and socially.

Again, the focus of God and His Kingdom is relationships. When He gave you the "power to create wealth," He gave you the ability to connect, love, and serve one another in ways that make your relationships stronger.

That is why the enemy attacks your relationships more than he attacks your finances. This is where your power is!

Jesus said the one distinction from the world His disciples would have is their love for one another. (See John 13:34-35.) Love includes the ability to transact with others in healthy, significant ways. This kind of love creates a flourishing environment for your God-given power to create wealth.

Bring It to the Next Level

God truly delights in working closely with you to make a huge impact on those you serve. Here is an expanded version of our definition of wealth:

Wealth is co-creating with God to "Wow!" others!

Wealth is co-creating with God to "Wow!" others!

Imagine God is right beside you with His elbow locked in yours, whispering secrets to you throughout the day. He wants your life to be an adventure regardless of where or what your work is.

"For we are . . . laborers together with . . . God" (1 Cor. 3:9 KJV).

An abundance-minded person comes into a relationship with the thought of how he or she is going to serve, bless, and "Wow!" the other person. Scarcity-driven people determine the value of a relationship only by what they can take or benefit from the relationship.

Which do you think people will be more attracted to? With which of these do you think God is more eager to work intimately?

Have you ever had a "Wow!" experience with someone? (To watch the "Wow!" story of when Tim met Sandy, go to Session 5 in the Corridor of Experts on www.PowerToCreate.org—you will enjoy it!)

It might have been the way your spouse or other relative surprised you with a party or special gift. Perhaps it was watching your children perform on a stage or athletic field. You may have had a "Wow!" experience from the way someone served you at a restaurant or while shopping.

Write down events in your life in which you had a "Wow!" moment:

1. _____

2. _____

3. _____

4. _____

5. _____

Write down events when you have caused others to say "Wow!":

1. _____

2. _____

3. _____

4. _____

5. _____

The Kingdom of God is the Kingdom of promotion. You get promoted when you live your life to "Wow!" people.

What I Like about You

One of the secrets of impacting people is to understand a key aspect of human nature. When someone likes you, what is it about you they like? Here is the secret: they like how they feel about themselves when they are with you.

Take inventory of your life right now. How do people feel about themselves when they are with you?

_____

_____

"Wow!" strategies include gifts from the heart and gifts from the hand. An embrace. A kind, encouraging, timely word. Giving a gift. Doing something with or for someone. Going the "extra mile" in the excellence of your work. It may be simply being present and emotionally connected with someone, spending focused, attentive time with him or her.

Understand that creating "Wow!" is a development process. Do not get discouraged as you begin to move outside of your comfort zone to impact people in significant ways. It is important to get started and stay with it!

Who in your life is desperate or deserving of a "Wow!" moment from you today?

Who in your life is desperate or deserving of a "Wow!" moment from you today? Who is the first person that comes to mind? What "Wow!" action do you want to take?

_____

_____

_____

Personal Application

Consider your work and the impact you are making with it. Listen to what God might be saying to you about creating a "Wow!" strategy for the people you work with and the customers you serve.

What "Wow!" strategy comes to mind?

_____

_____

_____

What are the first three steps you can take to implement this strategy?

1. _____

_____

2. _____

_____

3. _____

_____

Between You and God . . .

Dear Heavenly Father, thank You for the life of adventure You are calling me into! Thank You for giving me the power to create so that I can work intimately with You to "Wow!" the people You have called me to serve. Inspire within me "Wow!" strategies and actions that I can bring into my work and key relationships. Help me move with focus and courage to implement these ideas starting today.

Capture Your Learning

Please consider the following as you journal:

❑ What became very clear to you during this session that you can apply practically to your life?

❑ Do you sense God's excitement to work with and through you to "Wow!" others?

❑ How is God working within you to expand the borders of your work and the value you create?

_____

_____

Corridor of the Experts

Get additional insights from Tim and other experts at

www.PowerToCreate.org

Notes from the Expert Videos:

In our next session, we are going to tap into a number of strategies that will help us boost our productivity levels!

Answers to the Companion Exercise for Video Session 5

1. purpose
2. enjoyment
3. intimately
4. connection
5. intense
6. faith
7. borders
8. Mentor
9. others
10. "Wow!"

POWER TO CREATE

Unlock Greater Purpose, Relationships & Finances

First be fruitful in the little, THEN multiply. If you don't, you may multiply dysfunction and unlearned lessons.

—Tim Redmond

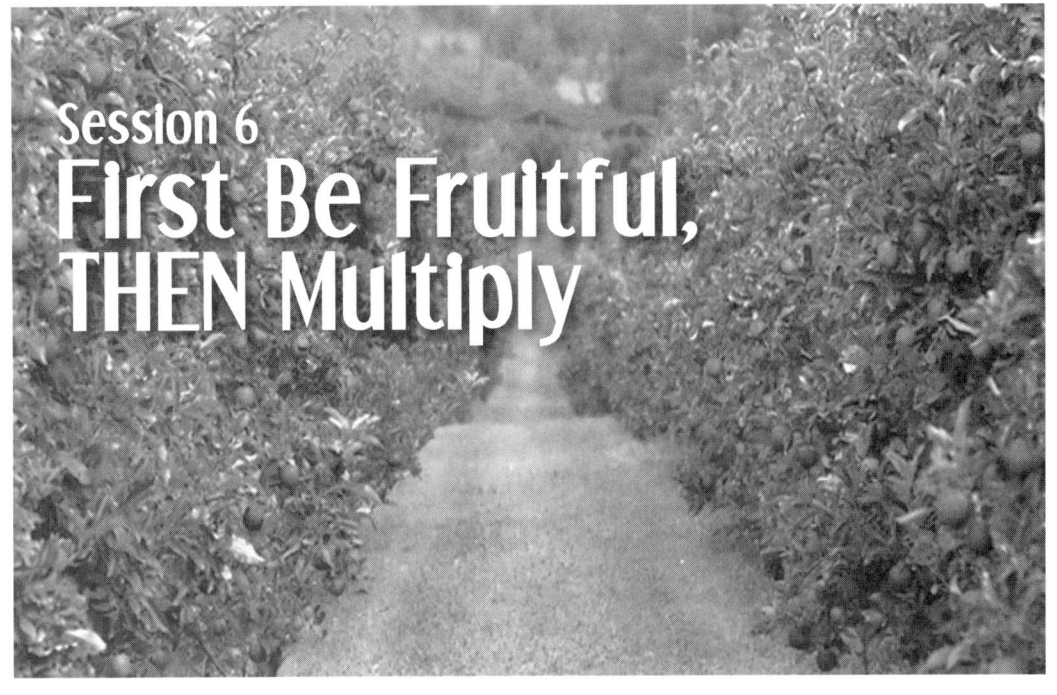

Session 6

First Be Fruitful, THEN Multiply

PowerKeys . . .

❑ Discover important principles of productivity to apply in your life today.

❑ Find out why so many run away from their God-given opportunities; and instead, learn how you can embrace them.

❑ Master practical disciplines that will help you accelerate your capacity to create value.

Companion Exercise for Video Session 6

1. Studies show that about _____ of people go to their graves having never fulfilled their purpose.

2. The pattern of the Kingdom is to start _____.

3. If we don't become fruitful first, we will multiply dysfunction and _____ lessons.

4. The "fruitful stage" is really the _____ stage.

5. Don't skip through the "fruitful" stage and move right into the "_____" stage.

6. The lack of follow _____ and follow _____ are among the biggest enemies to your success.

7. The *Power to Create* flows from _____.

8. _____ is a predominant emotional state of the Kingdom of God.

9. The opposite of learning is _____.

10. The pathway of blaming will _____ you and paralyze the gift God has given you.

My Notes from Video Session 6:

My Notes from Video Session 6:

Personal Discovery

"And God blessed them, and God said unto them, Be fruitful, and multiply, and replenish the earth, and subdue it: and have dominion over the fish of the sea, and over the fowl of the air, and over every living thing that moveth upon the earth" (Gen. 1:28 KJV).

In the book of Genesis, God mentioned "be fruitful and multiply" more frequently than anything else. This is not just referring to growing a family; it is also referring to being productive as Jesus mentioned in John 15.

On our journey as wealth-creators, we have to learn to overcome internal and external obstacles. The challenges include our thought processes on the inside and the relationships, finances, and unexpected events on the outside.

As we unpack the principles of productivity in this session, we are going to gain energy and perspective when the going gets tough.

As we unpack the principles of productivity in this session, we are going to gain energy and perspective when the going gets tough. Success and wealth creation are not for the faint of heart. It takes tremendous inner fortitude to grow and overcome.

Studies show that about 80 percent of people reach the end of their lives feeling they have not fulfilled their purpose. Implementing these keys will help you be in the 20 percent of those who do fulfill their purpose and help others do the same.

Start Small, Grow Fast

The first key to productivity is this: the pattern of the Kingdom is to start small.

When pursuing your purpose, start the process of being fruitful, multiplying, replenishing, and subduing by taking little steps. It is in the little steps that you learn crucial knowledge, develop skills, and gain confidence.

Being consistent with little steps will lead to big steps and big results (like it did with the Pancake Lady). It is the process of learning, adjusting, and THEN growing fast!

Looking back on your experiences. Have you followed this first principle? Write down one or two examples that come to mind.

_____

_____

_____

> *They want "the big" right now without going through the development steps to prepare them to handle "the big."*

This is where so many miss it. They want "the big" right now without going through the development steps to prepare them to handle "the big." Success looks so attractive that we want it immediately. What does not look attractive is the price required to achieve it. This is why so many people run away from the very opportunity that was designed to cause them to multiply.

Overnight success is rarely reached overnight. Do not be afraid of the smallness of the beginning; be willing to do whatever it takes.

Think of the thousands of cookies Mrs. Fields served to grocery store managers from the trunk of her car before her business blasted off. Hewlett-Packard started in a garage, as have many other amazing businesses and ministries!

What is the desire you dream of reaching? Keep your vision clearly in mind as you take the hundreds of little steps that lead to "the big" of your dream.

As the prophet warned, "Do not despise these small beginnings, for the LORD rejoices to see the work begin" (Zech. 4:10 NLT). God is rejoicing over you because you have begun!

What is the Lord leading you to start now that you have been putting off?

What specific action are you going to take now to get started with what you wrote above?

Now examine the actions you wrote above. Did you remember the principle of "start small"? Re-write these below, breaking them into even smaller action steps.

Whom are you going to ask to hold you accountable to help keep your "hand to the plow" in the beginning days?

What Are You Multiplying?

The second key to productivity states: if we do not first become fruitful before multiplying, we will multiply dysfunction and unlearned lessons.

We want to skip through the "fruitful" stage and move right into the "multiply stage." Yet rushing through this phase means you might run past valuable skill and relationship development that is essential for becoming fruitful in your work.

The fruitful stage can be messy.

The fruitful stage can be messy. In many cases, it involves years of testing dozens of approaches, making mistakes, and implementing adjustments before discovering what really works and what does not.

It is a time when you may feel stuck and seem to be making no progress. The lessons learned appear to be costing more than they are worth. It is at this stage you may be tempted to give up.

Consider two captains of their industries: J.C. Penny and Walt Disney. They overcame bankruptcies, nervous breakdowns, impossibilities in funding their visions—yet they did not give up. After being knocked down, they got back up and moved forward with a new approach.

Learning to be fruitful is making sure your growth and investment does not exceed your education.

Learning to be fruitful is making sure your growth and investment does not exceed your education.

For instance, an investor friend was doing very well with a certain type of investment. As he began to grow and amass huge amounts of cash, he started to get restless with his core business. He started dabbling with other kinds of investments he was familiar with but had not yet mastered.

He fell into a trap that catches so many. In his excitement of obtaining excess cash and growth, he forgot about the importance of using restraint. Driven by his emotions instead of business disciplines, he invested too much money too quickly into a new market he didn't know that much about. He lost hundreds of thousands of dollars.

I have also seen the "growing beyond education" mistake with business owners wanting to expand their business too quickly. They think they can "expand" their way from losing money to becoming profitable by opening up new locations or product lines. This approach rarely works. Start small and grow to a place of strength and profitability, THEN add new locations and product lines based on the wisdom you have acquired.

Multiple Streams of Income

"Multiplying before fruitfulness" occurs frequently with individuals who set up multiple streams of income. Is having several sources of income a great idea? Absolutely! Then why does it rarely work?

Here is what typically happens: with enthusiasm, people pursue an income opportunity. After trying to make it work, the first income stream does not appear to be producing much income. They find another opportunity and apply their usual work style and habits. Unfortunately, these include bad habits and unlearned lessons.

The process keeps repeating because they are multiplying mediocrity in each stream. The lack of success usually is not because the product or pay structure was faulty; rather, it was because they have not learned and applied the basic business disciplines needed to make any of the streams profitable.

The lack of success usually is not because the product or pay structure was faulty; rather, it was because they have not learned and applied the basic business disciplines needed to make any of the streams profitable.

Apply These Business Disciplines

What are some of the basic business disciplines I am referring to? Here are six of them:

1. **Make your purpose clear and compelling.** It answers the question, "Why are you doing what you are doing?"

2. **Clarify your most important activities and spend most of your time on them.** Increase clarity when planning each week and day by identifying and implementing one to three of the most important tasks to accomplish during that period. Do not allow low-payoff activities to dominate your day by mistaking activity for productivity. Lack of focus kills productivity.

A lack of perceived value and creativity will repel the very people you want to attract!

3. **Invest in your knowledge and skill to become successful in your specific business.** This is a key to projecting value and instilling confidence in others towards you. A lack of perceived value and creativity will repel the very people you want to attract!

4. **Follow up on items and people in a timely manner.** Sloppy follow-up is one of the biggest enemies of your growth and success.

5. **Follow through to the finish.** Leaving a trail of unfinished projects and phone calls drains your power to create, projects unreliability, and robs you of attracting more rewarding opportunities.

6. **Manage cash and credit properly.** Do not spend what you do not have. Learn to move forward creatively regardless of your cash level. Use credit with wisdom or even as a last resort. (Sometimes "easy cash" makes for stupid spending.)

Of these six disciplines, which of these are the strongest in your life? Why?

With which of these six disciplines do you have the most challenge? Why?

_____

_____

_____

What is one step you are going to take this week to strengthen this discipline in your life?

_____

_____

_____

Being faithful in the little leads to the capacity to handle much more as denoted in Luke 16:10. Becoming faithful is a process of developing your hands (skills) and heart (discernment, sound decision making). Mastering these six disciplines is what the fruitful stage is all about.

Where Power Flows

The third key to productivity is: the *Power To Create* flows from learning.

Products and services are constantly changing and being replaced. What is more important in the wealth-creation process is WHAT you learn and WHOM you meet.

Learning involves more than just gaining information. Information is helpful but does not have power within itself to create transformation. The world is overflowing with access to more information than at any other time in history. But is the world significantly better off because of it?

True learning is not focused as much on gaining knowledge as it is on changing your images—what you see and how you see it.

True learning is not focused as much on gaining knowledge as it is on changing your images—what you see and how you see it.

Have you ever declared, "This message changed my life!" When you said that, what actually changed in your life? Do you still have the same relatives, friends, and challenges? Of course! So what changed?

You changed HOW you look at what you are looking at. Success is a process of improving your "looks"! It is not what you look like in the mirror but how you look at what you are looking at.

Strongholds are the wrong images that contradict God's thoughts.

The apostle Paul said we are in a war, and the weapons in this war are not your typical weapons. However, they are powerful enough to pull down the stronghold of your enemy in the war. What is the war all about? He made that clear in this passage. It is casting down imaginations. The strongholds are the wrong images that contradict God's thoughts. (See 2 Cor. 10:3-5 KJV.)

That is why the second of the Ten Commandments warns us about not having graven or wrong images of God. (See Ex. 20:4.) An inaccurate, distorted image of God will blur how we look at ourselves. Why? Because we are made in the image of God. (See Gen. 1:26.)

Learning means changing how you look at yourself and your situations. The *Power to Create* equips you to:

1. Implement your idea.

2. Evaluate the results.

3. Make adjustments to get better results.

4. Keep repeating steps two and three forever.

These four powerful steps are the "learning process" in action! To learn means to be willing to challenge the status quo and change the thoughts you think and actions you take.

Consider the way my son Joshua responded as a five-year-old entrepreneur running his lemonade stand. As I stated in the Video Session, when he realized customers were not coming to him, he made an adjustment to get better results. He carried his lemonade TO the customers and came back with a pocket full of money!

> *To learn means to be willing to challenge the status quo and change the thoughts you think and actions you take.*

As Henry Blackaby said in his book, *Experiencing God*, "If you join God in what He is doing, you must make adjustments. You cannot stay where you are and move on with God at the same time."

Think about experiences where you have been successful. What are some of the most important lessons you have learned that helped you succeed?

1. _____

2. _____

3. _____

True learning involves an adjustment you make in thought and/or action. With each of the lessons you listed above, what adjustment did you make in your life that shows that you learned the lesson.

1. _____

2. _____

3. _____

Cast Not Away Your Confidence

Making adjustments may feel unnerving at times. You may feel overwhelmed or weighed down by the results not improving as fast as you want to see.

Jesus encouraged us to "learn from Him." (See Matt. 11:28-30.) The way He looks at results and change may be different from the way you are looking at them. How did He stay in peace when adjustments were needed? Ask yourself how Jesus would prepare for and approach issues you are facing.

> *Jesus looked at everything from a place of possibility. He walked with confidence. He assumed success when He faced a challenge.*

Jesus looked at everything from a place of possibility. He walked with confidence. He assumed success when He faced a challenge. Walking in confidence is walking with a heart of faith and certainty that you will achieve positive results— even if it involves change.

Does that mean you will always have the results you envision? Probably not. However, when you maintain confidence (which is built on skills, relationships, and direction from God), it improves your probability of success. Your confidence will keep you focused and committed long enough to reach the goals you are working for.

Do you walk in confidence and the attitude of "assume success" when you begin a task?

What are some things you can do to strengthen your confidence?

_____

_____

_____

_____

The Enemy of Learning

Since learning is so important in the *Power to Create* process, the last key to productivity in this session will identify the opposite of learning.

The opposite of learning is blaming.

The pathway of blaming will destroy you and paralyze the gift that God has given you. Learning is the pathway of prosperity; blaming is the pathway of poverty.

Learners look inward to make adjustments. In opposition to learning, blamers look outward to make excuses. Leaders are learners who first go inward before they go outward in dealing with issues. Victims first go outward and blame.

> *Learners look inward to make adjustments. In opposition to learning, blamers look outward to make excuses.*

When playing the role of a victim, people will not have the perspective to properly value their experiences. Their experiences are commonly looked at negatively, which blinds them from seeing anything positive in their present or future. A victim's past dominates his present and future.

It is just the opposite with victors. They see all of their experiences, including setbacks, as equipping them to create better, faster, and more creatively.

Looking back at your experiences, in what situations did you respond as a victim or as a victor?

_____

_____

_____

_____

I urge you not to conform to the culture of blamers. They deny responsibility and choose the ineffective treadmill of blaming. Do you remember from the Video Session what my son Joshua said after hitting his older brother with the Buzz Lightyear doll? "It wasn't me, it was my hand!"

How are you responding to the people and situations in your life right now? Are you blaming or learning?

_____

_____

_____

What Causes the Damage?

> *What happens to you is not as damaging as how you interpret what happens to you.*

Here is a profound reality relating to negative experiences. What happens to you is not as damaging as how you interpret what happens to you. It is what that experience means to you.

For instance, if your business or marriage failed, your interpretation could be that you are a failure. You blame yourself and others.

One of the big challenges you will have to overcome on the journey of success is learning how to change a painful event from a blaming to a learning experience. Giving yourself permission to change the meaning of a situation is one of the first steps to healing and empowerment.

In what current situations could you be blaming instead of learning?	Instead of blaming, what lesson can you learn from this?

Blaming can involve forces beyond our control like the weather, economy, and to some degree, politics. Blaming also frequently involves other people.

Whom are you blaming right now? (This may involve something that happened years ago but still affects you.)

_____

_____

_____

Why are you blaming them, and how is that helping you create value now?

_____

_____

_____

What life-giving lessons can you draw from your experience with that person?

_____

_____

_____

How can you look at those experiences with gratitude for the lessons they helped you learn, and how can you express your gratitude to the people involved?

_____

_____

_____

Move from blaming to learning.

Personal Application

What is one area in your life or work that is not as fruitful as you would like it to be?

_____

_____

_____

_____

What skill and/or mindset is needed to help you become more fruitful?

_____

_____

_____

_____

One of the keys to fruitfulness is being able to measure your results and progress in practical, easy-to-follow ways. How will you know you have become "fruitful" in this area? Include a measured target you are shooting for and when you want to reach that target.

_____

_____

_____

Between You and God . . .

Dear Heavenly Father, You desire that I become fruitful and multiply. Thank You for equipping me with the ability to become very fruitful in the purpose You called me to fulfill. I come to learn from You and ask for Your help to develop the disciplines needed in any areas of my life that are not productive. Thank You for Your amazing grace, which is empowering me now to be fruitful and multiply in this one area (*list area*: _____)
you have gifted me to address!

Capture Your Learning

Please consider the following as you journal:

❑ For everything God expects from you, He also equips you to produce. Envision yourself very successful and living out your God-given assignment. What are you doing?

❑ What did you learn about yourself when you shifted from blaming to learning? (And regarding the situations and people you listed in the Workbook exercises above.)

❑ What became very clear to you during this session that you can apply practically to your life?

_____

_____

Corridor of the Experts

Get additional insights from Tim and other experts at

www.PowerToCreate.org

(Be sure to watch Tim's video on why so many Jews are successful and another video covering the productivity key of "Wealth Flows from Motion, Poverty Flows from Procrastination.")

Notes from the Expert Videos:

_____

_____

_____

_____

_____

_____

In our next session, we are going to unveil key details in the gift He has imparted to each one of us!

Answers to the Companion Exercise for Video Session 6

1. 80 percent
2. small
3. unlearned
4. messy
5. multiply
6. up, through
7. learning
8. Confidence
9. blaming
10. destroy

POWER TO CREATE

Unlock Greater Purpose, Relationships & Finances

The size of the problem you solve determines the size of the reward.

—Tim Redmond

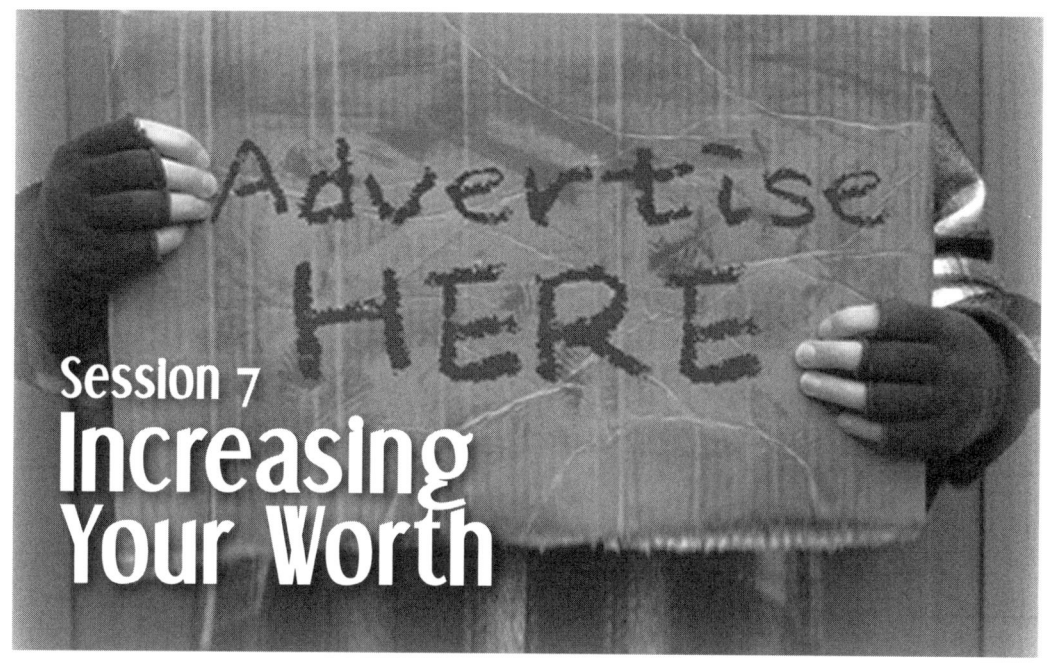

Session 7
Increasing Your Worth

PowerKeys . . .

❑ Incorporate the key principles for increasing your worth and the rewards they attract.

❑ Determine what systems in your life are working and which are not.

❑ Implement the key that will attract more promotion, customers, influence, and profits.

Companion Exercise for Video Session 7

1. Your success is connected to someone else's _____.

2. The size of the problems you solve determines the size of the _____.

3. Putting ALL of your heart into your work sets you up for _____.

4. How you do anything is how you do _____.

5. Wealth flows out of great, well-organized systems; poverty flows out of _____ systems.

6. Weeds choke the productivity and _____ of the garden.

7. _____ left to itself tends toward disorganization, chaos, and some form of poverty.

8. When you do ANY work, first be the worker, then be the _____.

9. What you don't maintain, you will _____.

10. Be on _____.

    _____ what you say.

    _____ what you start.

    _____ others.

My Notes from Video Session 7:

My Notes from Video Session 7:

Personal Discovery

In God's value system, your worth is not based on what you do or what you have but on His extravagant generosity towards you through the liberating work of Jesus Christ. Once you truly understand His captivating love and enthusiastic acceptance of you, it can become the foundation of your confidence and ability to create value.

There is nothing you can do or not do that will reduce your worth to God. His love for you is the beginning and end of your entire journey.

He put His greatness in you as a seed. A seed becomes a tree through a development process. It is the same with you!

At the same time, God loves growth! He put His greatness in you as a seed. A seed becomes a tree through a development process. It is the same with you! God wants you to grow in your ability to create value.

That is why the focus of this session is to help you create ever increasing levels of value by working intimately with God. In this context, value means worth.

As it relates to your development process, your "worth" is based on the perceived value you project. Others have to see what you do and create as worth their time, attention, or money.

Their Problem—My Opportunity!

Your success is connected to someone else's problem. Your opportunity to create value is attached to someone else's disappointment or frustrations AND your ability to solve that problem. The size or difficulty of the problem you solve determines the reward you attract. The key is making your "worth" more worthwhile.

For instance, when the Pancake Lady first started making pancakes, her customers perceived they were good, so they bought them. As she began experimenting with her recipe, she produced pancakes they loved and could not be without! Then she made various pastries available and added a catering service. Over time, the value she offered to her customers increased, so they did not mind paying higher prices. They purchased even more of her products. Her sales exploded in growth as a result.

Please note that no work or effort is insignificant in the Kingdom of God. Never diminish or despise the work you are currently doing (as long it is respecting God, others, and yourself).

Your work is a noble place where you release your worship to God and demonstrate His creative compassion through you to others!

Your work is a noble place where you release your worship to God and demonstrate His creative compassion through you to others!

This session will cover three key principles that will help you create increasing levels of worth.

The Principle of "ALL"

The first "Increasing Your Worth" principle, the principle of "ALL," is simply putting all of your heart into what you do.

The anchor scripture is Colossians 3:23: "And whatever you do, do it heartily, as to the Lord and not to men." This verse tells you HOW to work: "heartily," meaning with ALL of your heart! It also tells you WHY you work. "As unto the Lord" means working as if the Lord is your employer and He will be directly affected by the quality of work you do.

When you work with only half of your heart involved, you may wonder where the presence of God is in your work. As a result, you may feel dissatisfied and discouraged with your work.

That is why God wants you to show up fully engaged! This is NOT saying you have to be possessed and controlled by your work. It is healthy to create boundaries between your work and time with your family and friends.

However, when you go to work, bring your whole heart with you. Make your work a signature of excellence that demonstrates you and God co-creating together. Be like the Grocery Store Lady mentioned in the Video Session and put ALL of your heart into your work to set in motion your creative capacities.

How you do anything is how you do everything.

Check Your Heart Rate

Using a scale from 1 to 10 with 1 being "I put no heart into my work" and 10 being "I put all of my heart into my work," how would you rate the "heartiness" of your work? Circle your answer below:

1   2   3   4   5   6   7   8   9   10

Why did you give yourself that rating?

_____

_____

_____

What is one practical action you can take to increase the "heartiness" of your work?

_____

_____

_____

Systems Drive Success

The second "Increasing Your Worth" principle is establishing success through the systems you set up and continually improve.

Systems are simply the way things are consistently done. There are good systems and bad systems. Even if you have not formally set up a system around an activity like sales, cash management, and education, a system still has been created by default.

Wealth flows from great, well-organized systems. Poverty flows from chaotic, poorly defined systems.

Wealth flows from great, well-organized systems. Poverty flows from chaotic, poorly defined systems.

To increase your worth, it is important to look at the health of the systems in your personal and professional life. And before you dismiss this topic because you do not like system-related discussions, consider the following:

God loves systems!

He built the whole universe around systems. The Law of Harvest ("what you sow is what you reap" as described many times in the Bible) is a system. The relationship of sun, planets, and stars is called a solar system. Even our own bodies are comprised of systems such as the respiratory, nervous, and digestive systems. All of God's creation reflects systems.

The degree of wealth or poverty in our lives many times has to do with the effectiveness of the systems we set up and maintain in our lives.

I was consulting a businessman who asked me to help him grow his business from five million to twenty-five million dollars. My response was, "Sure, I have helped many businesspeople with this and I would love to help you!" One of the first things I looked at was the effectiveness of his systems. Were his systems producing a healthy profit?

His business was losing several hundred thousand dollars each year. As we began to evaluate his business, he terminated our relationship. Sadly, he was unwilling to address his faulty systems and continued to struggle.

Systems of Abundance

God created "systems of abundance" when He created the heavens and the earth. "Then God said, 'Let the land sprout with vegetation—every sort of seed-bearing plant, and trees that grow seed-bearing fruit. These seeds will then produce the kinds of plants and trees from which they came.' And that is what happened" (Gen. 1:11 NLT).

Since you are made in God's image (to operate like Him), you are to set up systems of abundance in all that you create. The concept of "First Be Fruitful, THEN Multiply" as discussed in the previous session revolves around creating systems that produce abundance.

Since you are made in God's image (to operate like Him), you are to set up systems of abundance in all that you create.

Here are some of the common systems people set up in their personal lives and businesses:

❏ Education System: investing in the skill development of yourself and your staff

❏ Decision-Making System: handling ideas, making decisions, and communicating them to others

❏ Planning Systems: goal achievement and ongoing planning

❏ Marketing and Sales: how you and your staff project your company and persuade customers to keep buying

❏ Information Systems: what you gather, evaluate, and use to make decisions

❏ Cash-Flow Management: when and how to invest and spend

Of the systems listed above (or another system that comes to mind), what is your best-running system? Why?

_____

_____

_____

Which of these systems is the least productive? Why?

_____

_____

_____

What is one step you are going to take this week to strengthen this system in your life or business?

_____

_____

_____

Tend the Garden

Anything (organizations, relationships, even our own bodies) left to themselves tend toward disorganization, chaos, and some form of poverty.

The first task God assigned to Adam was to tend the garden. "Then the LORD God took the man and put him in the garden of Eden to tend and keep it" (Gen. 2:15).

If you do not tend a garden, it will be overgrown with weeds. Weeds choke the productivity and purpose of the garden.

Anything (organizations, relationships, even our own bodies) left to themselves tend toward disorganization, chaos, and some form of poverty.

Think of a relationship that you have invested in and tended well. What are some of the benefits you are enjoying because of your diligence with this relationship?

_____

_____

Is there a relationship that comes to mind that you have not tended well? Why haven't you done so, and what do you plan to do about it?

_____

_____

_____

Besides relationships, is there something that you have tended well? What specific things did you do to "tend this garden"?

_____

_____

_____

Making Sure It Is Good

When you are creating, evaluating, and improving the systems in your life, there is one very important concept to consider. It is mentioned seven times in the first chapter of Genesis.

After each act of God's creation, it says, "And God saw it was good." (See Gen. 1:4, 10, 12, 18, 21, 25, 31.)

This phrase puzzled me. I thought to myself, "Of course it was good! God is perfect, and He created it."

Scripture is given to display and reveal the nature of God. It is also given to show us a pattern to apply to our lives. Here is the lesson: when you create or do anything, make sure that it is good!

Genesis 1:12 reveals this truth clearly in the _Amplified Bible:_ "And God saw that it was good (suitable, admirable) and He approved it." He made sure it was suitable for the situation and made it with such excellence that it was admirable. After He made it, He pulled back and looked it over carefully and then approved it.

Jesus followed that pattern when healing a blind man.

"Then He came to Bethsaida; and they brought a blind man to Him, and begged Him to touch him. So He took the blind man by the hand and led him out of the town. And when He had spit on his eyes and put His hands on him, He asked him if he saw anything. And he looked up and said, 'I see men like trees, walking.' Then He put His hands on his eyes again and made him look up. And he was restored and saw everyone clearly" (Mark 8:22-25.)

This is the process of making sure you "see to it to make sure it is good."

First Be the Worker, Then the Boss

I teach my children the "see that it is good" principle since it affects every-thing they do. Frequently, I remind them, "Make sure your work is suitable, admirable, and has your stamp of approval on it."

To help my kids apply this powerful principle, I gave them this metaphor: when you do ANY work, first be the worker, then be the boss. Complete the task as a worker, then pull back, review your work as if you are the boss, and make sure it is stamped with your approval.

Do you remember from the Video Session the satisfaction I had when one of my sons finally applied this to mowing the lawn?

Think of a time that you implemented "First Be the Worker, Then the Boss" principle. What did you do, and how did you feel after you completed it?

_____

_____

_____

The "Making Sure It Is Good" principle is illustrated in Proverbs 27:23: "Be thou diligent to know the state of thy flocks, and look well to thy herds" (KJV). The *New Living Translation* of this verse clarifies it further, "Know the state of your flocks, and put your heart into caring for your herds."

The opposite of diligence is casualness. Consider this: casualness creates casualties.

The opposite of diligence is casualness. Consider this: casualness creates casualties.

Have you suffered casualties because of casualness? Describe an experience where this happened and what you learned from it.

_____

_____

_____

_____

What you don't maintain, you will lose. This applies to everything in life: finances, possessions, and especially relationships!

Make sure your work represents the excellence of royalty because that is who you are!

Contagiously Referable

The third "Increasing Your Worth" principle is this: make yourself contagiously referable.

The more reliable you and your creations become, the more people will trust you. Trust increases the quality and quantity of your transactions.

Your capacity to increase your worth is tied to the relationships you establish. The more reliable you and your creations become, the more people will trust you. This will cause them to want to continue interacting with you and investing in your products and services. Trust increases the quality and quantity of your transactions.

Prolonged prosperity is built on character because character is the basis for trust and credibility.

The key to the *Power to Create* is building your life on the character of Christ. This is what Paul prayed in Galatians 4:19, ". . .until Christ is formed in you."

A few years ago, a friend of mine opened his own auto repair shop after working for years as a mechanic for a dealership in town. I knew he possessed the key traits that make a business succeed: character, reliability, and skill. His word was his bond, and he stood by all of his work.

Though it is a relatively new business, he just passed the million-dollar mark with no signs of slowing down. With all of the people my wife and I have referred to him, I have not heard one hint of dissatisfaction. People trust and love him. He has mastered the keys of becoming contagiously referable.

So, how do you become contagiously referable?

Being referred by those who have had a "Wow!" experience with you is one of best ways to increase your worth. Referrals are built on character. People become walking billboards for you because of the trustworthy, consistent ways you manage your responsibilities.

> *People become walking billboards for you because of the trustworthy, consistent ways you manage your responsibilities.*

Here are four habits that will help build your character and the proven reliability others will grow to trust:

1. **Be on time.** This shows you respect yourself and whom you are meeting. It is a small act that casts a big shadow of how much you can be trusted.

2. **Do what you say.** Your word most accurately reflects who you are. As you honor yourself by doing what you say, this builds the trust of others

towards you. Be careful to say only those things that you are commit-ted to do. Psalm 15:4 speaks of one who abides in God's presence: "He who swears to his own hurt and does not change." This verse and chapter describe you!

3. **Finish what you start.** This is a powerful character carver that demands focus, organization, and commitment to see a task through to its completion. If you become famous for finishing what you start, do you think people will want to refer others to you?

4. **Celebrate others.** Being imprisoned by a mindset of scarcity, many cannot see beyond their own need and pain. Celebrating others sincerely shifts the environment around you to make it attractive and inviting for others to enter. Don't make this more difficult than it is. Simply being polite and grateful are powerful ways of celebrating people.

Evaluate your refer-ability. Think of customers you attract and people who request your insights and help. What percentage of new relationships would you estimate comes by referrals from others?

_____%

Are you pleased with that percentage? Explain.

_____

_____

_____

Which of these four "contagious refer-ability" factors are most evident in your life? Why?

_____

_____

Which of these most needs your attention? How can you improve it?

_____

_____

_____

As you begin to operate in these principles of increasing your worth, you are setting the stage for significant progress in your life!

Personal Application

Evaluate the systems in your life and/or business. Think of a "Wow!" strategy that you noted in Session 5 ("Relationships that Produce 'Wow!'").

What system most helps you to implement that "Wow!" strategy?

_____

_____

What are three things you can do to make that system better geared to "Wow!" your family, friends, or customers?

1. _____

_____

2. _____

_____

3. _____

_____

Between You and God . . .

Dear Heavenly Father, thank You for investing so much into me. Help me to understand the extent of Your love for me, so it becomes the immoveable foundation for my confidence and the development of the gifts You have given me to impact others. Help me to think like You do about systems. Give me wisdom and insight to build and maintain "systems of abundance" so that I can create ever-increasing levels of value. Thank You for forming within me a greater expression of Christ's character that causes people to refer others to me. I am amazed at Your work within me and give You the glory and honor for all the good in my life!

Capture Your Learning

Please consider the following as you journal:

❏ Think of your worth and your ability to create value from the enthusiastic, loving heart of God.

❏ From the three principles shared in this session, how is God working on your character to implement these into your work?

❏ What became very clear to you during this session that you can apply practically to your life?

Corridor of the Experts

Get additional insights from Tim and other experts at
www.PowerToCreate.org

Notes from the Expert Videos:

\

_____

_____

_____

_____

_____

_____

_____

In our next session, we are going to unveil key details in the gift He has imparted to each one of us!

Answers to the Companion Exercise for Video Session 7
1. problem
2. reward
3. promotion
4. everything
5. chaotic
6. purpose
7. Anything
8. boss
9. lose
10. time, Do, Finish, Celebrate

POWER TO CREATE
Unlock Greater Purpose, Relationships & Finances

Successful people constantly look for opportunities to invest.

—Tim Redmond

Session 8

Start Creating Now–
Proven Strategies

PowerKeys . . .

❏ Implement a number of powerful, Kingdom-focused investment strategies to build wealth and increase your capacity to enrich the lives of others.

❏ Discover how investment strategies begin with investing in yourself and developing an educational plan for your growth.

❏ Learn the best way to eliminate debt quickly.

Companion Exercise for Video Session 8

1. Borrowing is taking from the future to have in the present. Investing is taking from the _____ to have in the future.

2. Strategy #1 — Invest First in _____ and Your Capacity to Create.

3. Strategy #2 — Work on Your Business and Income Sources _____ You Focus on Your Lifestyle.

4. Strategy #3 — Be a Generous _____.

5. Giving is an active, intimate form of _____.

6. God's reward to you is more responsibility and _____; in other words, He will give you a greater capacity to create and serve others.

7. Strategy #4 — Be a _____.

8. Savings is a _____ or manifestation of the mindset of abundance.

9. Strategy #5 — Multiply Your Savings by Establishing and Growing a _____ Investment Account.

10. Grow wealth by creating a profitable _____ or investing in one.

My Notes from Video Session 8:

My Notes from Video Session 8:

Personal Discovery

Successful people invest.

They are abundance-minded and want to create ever-increasing levels of value by constantly looking for opportunities to invest. Investors look to the future instead of being controlled by the past and present.

Investors look to the future instead of being controlled by the past and present.

Borrowing is taking from the future to have in the present. Investing is taking from the present to have in the future.

Now that you have a clearer understanding of the gift God gave you in Deuteronomy 8:18, you can focus on developing your own powerful investment mindsets and strategies.

The First Focus for Investing

The first investment strategy is this: invest first in yourself and your capacity to create.

Giving is what drives growth in the Kingdom of God. "Creating to serve" is a high form of giving. As you become more skillful at creating, your capacity to give increases along with it.

Investing in yourself means investing in YOUR education and learning experiences. Your journey through this curriculum is a great example of investing in yourself. Investing in yourself is one of the most unselfish things you can do.

In the name of "putting others first," some do not put value in investing in themselves. They are ready to invest in everyone and everything except themselves and their activities. In some cases, this reflects a lack of confidence, which can be a form of poverty.

In the name of "putting others first," some do not put value in investing in themselves.

One day a trusted banker told me, "Make sure most of your investment is in yourself." I didn't value what he said at that time. I went on to invest significantly in real estate and other businesses. I thought they were good investments and that they would help me multiply my money.

In fact, I did make good returns on several of the investments. However, when looking back, I realized that being so quick to invest in everything else but myself reflected a lack of confidence in my power to create value. I saw other investments as "more worthy" and neglected the main investment I was given stewardship over. In the end, I ended up losing several hundred thousand dollars and stifled my personal growth.

Looking first to put time and resources into other investments revealed how I had undervalued my ability to create. Yet this is the gift God wants most for us to invest in!

How would you rate your confidence level in your ability to create? (Circle one, 1 is no confidence, 10 is full confidence.)

1   2   3   4   5   6   7   8   9   10

Why did you give yourself that rating?

_____

_____

_____

What Is Your Education Plan?

As part of the ongoing employee-evaluation process at the software company I helped build, I required employees to create a personalized education plan for each year.

Here are some of the questions I wanted them to consider:

1. What strong points do you want to strengthen, and how do you plan to strengthen them?

2. What weaknesses and constraints are hindering your top performance, and how do you plan to reduce or eliminate their influence in your life?

3. What skills and wisdom do you want to develop that will help you become more productive in your current work AND towards your dreams beyond this job?

4. What classes, seminars, or conferences do you plan to attend within the next twelve months to help you with the three items above? If you haven't already, consider enrolling in my Accelerated Growth Coaching Program explained on page ____ or at www.PowerToCreate.org.

What books do you plan to read in the next 12 months?

5. What books do you plan to read in the next twelve months?

6. What mentors are speaking into your life, and how are you nurturing your relationships with them?

7. How are you capturing and recording ideas, strategies, and concepts that come to you during the year? (e.g., keep an Insights & Ideas Journal)

These are great questions for you to consider as well.

What are your educational plans for the next twelve months? Looking at the seven items above, give a brief planning response to each of them:

Strengths _____

_____

Constraints _____

_____

Skills _____

_____

Seminars _____

_____

Books _____

_____

Mentors _____

_____

Growth Journal _____

_____

When preparing your budget, be sure to allocate an amount for your Education Plan.

As you implement the principles in the *Power To Create* curriculum, you should expect to attract a greater cash flow into your life. How do you handle cash management from the mindset of a sound, Kingdom-focused investor? The remaining strategies answer this question.

Income and Lifestyle

Kingdom-minded investors focus on increasing their earnings to fulfill a higher purpose.

The second investment strategy puts the priority of working on your business and income sources BEFORE focusing on your desired lifestyle.

The quality of your lifestyle is a by-product of the value you produce. To their own hurt and anxiety, many spend in accordance with their desired lifestyle without considering their income level.

Before they know it, they are living far beyond their means without putting positive pressure on their income sources to support their lifestyle.

Kingdom-minded investors focus on increasing their earnings to fulfill a higher purpose. They work to increase their income above their lifestyle, so they can invest in their church and other Kingdom activities. They also use part of the excess to invest in solid investments (especially their own businesses!) to further expand their giving power.

The anchor verse for this strategy is Proverbs 24:27 NLT: "Do your planning and prepare your fields before building your house."

Looking at your past experience and current circumstances, how successful have you been at living this principle?

Do you want to increase your capacity to invest and give? You must break free from the pressures of a scarcity mindset screaming that you do not have enough. Establish the lifestyle you can support and live within those boundaries. As your capacity increases, you may choose to adjust your lifestyle as income allows.

Keep in mind that Kingdom-driven people make giving and investing a significant part of their lives. Always include those amounts in your planning and budgeting process.

Debt Elimination Strategy

A person buried with debt will find it very difficult to extravagantly give donations and build wealth the way he or she desires. If you want to fulfill your mandate to "have dominion" as stated in

A person buried with debt will find it very difficult to extravagantly give donations and build wealth the way he or she desires.

Genesis 1:28, taking dominion of your finances and getting rid of debt is a necessity.

It is important to reduce and eliminate every kind of debt in your life, especially debt on non-income-producing "lifestyle" assets such as furniture and "toys" purchased on credit. The difference between men and boys is the price of their toys. Although wives are frequently blamed for overspending, studies show the biggest financial challenges arise because of men's impulse purchases of high priced items.

To manage debt properly, you have to know exactly how your cash flow is coming and going. A convenient way to keep track of your cash flow is using a program such as Intuit's *Quicken* or Microsoft's *Money* that will import your bank, credit card, and investment transactions using the Internet.

If you have debt, learn to "snowball" the pay-down of your debt. "Snowball" refers to a way of maximizing your efforts on one debt at a time. Pay the largest payment possible each month to the lowest balance first, while making minimum payments on all the other debts. After the smallest debt is paid off, make maximum payments to the next lowest balance and so forth.

Understand that overcoming debt is a psychological battle as much as it is a cash management battle.

Understand that overcoming debt is a psychological battle as much as it is a cash management battle. That is why I recommend paying off the lowest balance first rather than attacking the debt with the highest interest rates. This approach allows you to experience victory in the short term, which will encourage you to stay with your overall debt reduction plan.

The success in this strategy is making the biggest debt payment each month against the lowest balance. When a debt is paid off, add that monthly payment amount to the payment amount of the next debt. For instance, let's say you are making $340 a month payment against the lowest balance. When that balance is paid off, add the full $340 amount to the payment you are making against the next debt. Do not look at the $340 as "extra income" you can spend; rather, keep applying it against the next smallest debt.

Before you know it, you will experience financial freedom with your cash flow and in your thoughts!

Power to Be Practical

Here are the steps to follow:

1. List all of your debts from the lowest balance on top to the highest balance on the bottom.

2. List the balance and minimum monthly payment and number of payments remaining based on making minimum payments.

3. Determine the "Extra Debt Payment" amount. This is the monthly payment amount you can add to the minimum payment of the smallest debt.

4. Create a new column for adjusted remaining payments based on adding the "Extra Debt Payment" amount and the accumulated debt payment as you pay off each loan.

Imagine that these are your debts:

Extra Debt Payment Amount: $300					
Debt Name	Balance	Minimum Payment	Snowball Payment	# of Remaining Payments	Adjusted # of Remaining Payments
Visa	$ 800	$ 40	$300+$40	25	3
Discover	$ 3,200	$ 150	$340+$150	27	Begin after Visa is paid
Car	$ 13,400	$ 360	$490+$360	44	Begin after Disc is paid
House	$205,000	$1200	$850+1200	324	Begin after Car is paid
Totals	$222,400	$1750			

You are already making $1750 each month to make the minimum monthly payments. In this example, you have determined that you want to add an extra $300 monthly payment against your debt until it is completely paid off. That means you will make $2050 ($1750 minimum payment + $300 extra debt payment) each month until all of your debt is paid off.

By following this debt reduction "snowball" payment plan, the first three debts listed above will be paid off almost two years early!

Please fill out this debt reduction chart using your numbers:

Extra Debt Payment Amount:					
Debt Name	Balance	Minimum Payment	Snowball Payment	# of Remaining Payments	Adjusted # of Remaining Payments
Totals					

As you adopt these disciplines into your life, you will have more freedom to give and invest.

Secrets of a Generous Giver

Abundance-minded people make giving a top priority with all of their earnings.

When you give money to your church or other worthy causes—especially with an empowered, joyful emotional state—it conditions your subconscious mind towards abundance. In other words, when actions are combined with intense emotions, you train yourself to think and behave in the way you desire.

This is why Paul said, "Don't copy the behavior and customs of this world, but let God transform you into a new person by changing the way you think. Then you will learn to know God's will for you, which is good and pleasing and perfect" (Rom. 12:2 NLT).

Here is how God wants us to think. "Honor the LORD with your possessions, and with the firstfruits of all your increase; so your barns will be filled with plenty, and your vats will overflow with new wine" (Prov. 3:9-10).

Giving is a way of acting and thinking like God. It is part of His DNA. "For God so loved the world that He gave . . ." (John 3:16). You are created in His image. You have His giving DNA!

Giving is a way of acting and thinking like God. It is part of His DNA.

When you give, it brings you into God's mindset of abundance and possibility. The act of giving programs you to see wealth and provisions in a never-ending, unlimited way. God is abundant, and you are abundant. Remind yourself of that every time you give cheerfully!

Being a consistent giver, even in difficult times, instills confidence within you because it reaffirms who your Source is. God created and owns everything. When you give back a portion, allow it to reinforce the reality that there is an intimate partnership between you and your Source.

Giving is a powerful form of worship. Based on the pattern revealed in the Old Testament, Jesus, our High Priest, takes what we give and offers it to our Heavenly Father as a form of worship.

"'And now, behold, I have brought the firstfruits of the land which you, O LORD, have given me.' Then you shall set it before the LORD your God, and worship before the Lᴏʀᴅ your God" (Deuteronomy 26:10). "One tenth of the produce of the land, whether grain from the fields or fruit from the

Money reveals and magnifies what is in your heart.

trees, belongs to the Lᴏʀᴅ and must be set apart to him as holy" (Lev. 27:30 NLT).

Money reveals and magnifies what is in your heart. That is why Jesus said, "For where your treasure is, there your heart will be also" (Matt. 6:21). Your treasure defines your heart's focus and priorities.

There is truth to discovering what a person's priorities are by looking at their checkbook. Another identifier is examining what comes out of your mouth when you are under pressure. As Jesus stated, "For out of the abundance of the heart the mouth speaks" (Matt. 12:34).

What do you frequently say when the subject of money is brought up?

_____

_____

_____

Put positive pressure on your giving, especially to your church. Take a moment to pray, be quiet within yourself, and hear how the Lord may be directing you. Be quick to obey what you hear.

If you were to increase your tithes and offerings in the next twelve months, how much could that be?

As a percent of your income: _____%

As an amount you give: $_____

I want to encourage you to constantly look for opportunities to give. Consider going beyond your tithes and offerings. When you see a need, especially in your own church, take care of it!

The Manifestation of Abundance

Effective investors are savers. The fourth strategy is just that: be a saver.

Some have looked at savings as a fear-driven activity, one that denotes a scarcity mindset or lack of faith. Actually, saving is just the opposite. Having the discipline to save is rooted in abundance.

Having the discipline to save is rooted in abundance.

Saving is a form of giving. It reinforces the mindset of abundance. Scarcity says you do not have enough right now; there is no way you can save. Abundance declares that you will figure out a way to save.

Saving is looking with expectation towards the future. It is the discipline to take from the present and move it to the future. It is actually the manifestation of the mindset of abundance.

When you begin to save, the action is more important than the amount!

Deuteronomy 28:8 says God will command a blessing on your storehouse. A modern-day storehouse can be a savings account. But how can He command a blessing on something that you have not set up?

When you begin to save, the action is more important than the amount!

When you set up your budget, I recommend you include an amount to be saved every time you receive earnings following the 10-10-80 allocation. Here are the details:

1. The first 10 percent is the tithe that belongs to the Lord. Bring it to your church.

2. The second 10 percent is to be put into a savings account. I recommend putting aside three to six months' worth of savings as the foundation before using savings for investment purposes. As your income increases, your tithes, offerings, and savings will increase. Be prepared to increase the percentage of savings beyond the 10 percent.

3. The remaining 80 percent is to cover everything else, including your obligations, personal-education investment, wants, and plans.

Some reasons for savings:

1. Emergency fund. Make your first goal to have one thousand dollars in this fund, then grow it to three to six months of your living expenses.

2. Long-term investments and wealth building.

3. Specific desires or projects like remodeling, a special vacation, or giving to a particular cause.

Remember, with cash you are positioned with power. You have more choices and can live more generously. Allow the Vietnamese Baker mentioned in the Video Session to inspire you to save!

Have you looked at savings as a fear-based activity? Why?

_____

_____

_____

Do you have a savings plan now? If or when you do, how will you compute how much to put into savings?

_____

_____

_____

What adjustments can you make that would allow you to begin to save or increase the amount you save?

_____

_____

_____

Multiply Your Savings

The fifth investment strategy is to multiply your savings.

After you stabilize your finances with an aggressive debt pay-down plan and saving beyond your emergency fund, it is time to begin growing a Wealth Investment Account (WIA).

This is an account dedicated to grow your capacity to create and give. It is taking some of your savings beyond the emergency fund amount to invest in growth opportunities like your business, the stock market, and real estate.

The idea of the WIA is to create a profitable business system or invest in one.

Treat this money as if it is your employee. Instead of you working for money, get money working for you. Again, I have found the investment that generates the highest return is when you put it into your own business or keep it in your control.

Allow your WIA to grow. Develop a plan that is measured in decades instead of just in years. As an investment generates income, pay the WIA back, so you continually have money to invest when the right opportunity becomes available.

Never be in a hurry when investing. As much as anything, it is a game of patience. James said when you let patience do its work, it leads you to a place where you are not lacking. (See James 1:4.)

The "investment of a lifetime" usually comes along every few weeks. Do not feel pressured that you will miss out if you do not act right now. When you feel that way, it is usually the voice of scarcity speaking to you.

The biggest investment mistakes I have experienced are when I invested beyond my education.

If you do not understand an investment, it is best not to participate. The biggest investment mistakes I have experienced are when I invested beyond my education, putting my money into opportunities that I knew little about. Countless other people have told me that this was their biggest mistake too.

On a video available only in the Bonus Material of the DVD Session 8, I share the Eight Guidelines for Investing. Although it is brief, it is packed full of practical information that can save you heartache, anxiety, and countless dollars lost in poor investments. While viewing it, I encourage you to take notes using the space provided at the end of this chapter.

Personal Application

How much more money would you like to give by the end of your life? (This is not just a wish but represents something that you could see yourself actually giving and you are willing to work towards its accomplishment.)

$_____

How much would you like to be giving on an annual basis?

$_____

How much would you like to have at retirement? (I do not believe in the concept of retirement but use the term to represent a point where 100 percent of your time is at your discretion.)

$_____

What practical steps can you take to help you reach these amounts? These may include getting out of debt in five years, taking classes to increase your skills for higher pay, and researching business opportunities (study and find a mentor to help you!).

1. _____

_____

2. _____
   _____

3. _____
   _____

4. _____
   _____

5. _____
   _____

Did you fill out the debt payment chart above? If not, take some time right now and take this important step towards wealth creation!

Between You and God . . .

Dear Heavenly Father, thank You for giving me the power to create wealth. It is such a precious and powerful gift to me. Help me to use this gift in a way that worships You. I ask for Your wisdom to apply all five of the investment strategies covered in this session. Help me to prioritize my spending and investing in a way that better reflects Your will for my life and causes me to significantly grow in the amounts I am able to give. Thank You for Your presence in my life. It is such an honor to co-create with You. I am enthusiastic about my future and know that You will lead me to live in a way that will be a great blessing to others and cause me to live with great joy.

Capture Your Learning

Please consider the following as you journal:

❑ As you evaluate your lifestyle in light of your purpose and God's Kingdom, what changes do you see yourself making?

❏ Wealth increases in an environment of discipline and creativity. How are you going to invite more of both into your life?

❏ What is the Lord speaking to you about the five investment strategies covered in this session?

Corridor of the Experts

Get additional insights from Tim and other experts at

www.PowerToCreate.org

Notes from the Expert Videos:

_____

_____

_____

_____

_____

_____

_____

_____

_____

Answers to the Companion Exercise for Video Session 8

1.   present
2.   Yourself
3.   Before
4.   Giver
5.   worship
6.   work
7.   Saver
8.   fruit
9.   Wealth
10. business

DO YOU NEED ADDITIONAL WORKBOOKS?

To order additional copies of the Power to Create Interactive Workbooks for group members, family, and friends, go to www.PowerToCreate.org and click on the "Order Now" button located on the Home page.

Once you have the order page on your screen, simply order the quantity of Workbooks that you desire. Please note that if you order 10 or more Workbooks at a time, you will receive a substantial discount. If you are ordering 10 or more Workbooks, be sure to order from the "10 or more Volume Discount" option.

If you have questions about ordering additional workbooks, please write, call or e-mail us:

> Redmond Leadership Institute
> PO Box 703052
> Tulsa, Oklahoma 74170
>
> 918.298.7766
>
> Contact @ redmondleadership.org

Please carefully review the following pages to tap into valuable additional resources that Tim and Sandy Redmond and the Redmond Leadership Institute team are making available to you to help you further unleash your unique *Power to Create . . .*

LIVE SEMINARS COMING TO YOU!

You will really enjoy having Tim come to your church or conference to provide his life-changing, humorous seminars live and in color! Here are his three most popular seminars:

Power to Create LIVE

The *Power to Create* LIVE is a transformational experience for the whole congregation! Clarify purpose, master money, and strengthen relationships. Walk away with practical tools. Tailor this LIVE seminar for an evening or Saturday seminar.

Power to Create Advanced Seminars

Grow businesses and increase giving with these advanced seminars. Perfect for church staff, owners, employees, entrepreneurs, and those interested in getting started in business. Delve deeper into the *Power to Create* principles in these seminars. Get specific business growth questions addressed. Ask about "quantum leap" coaching options that may be available with this seminar.

Transform Leaders Now! Seminar

This is a high impact, interactive leadership seminar that wakes up and mobilizes the leadership potential within the hearts of all who attend. It will clarify purpose, remove personal constraints, and equip the participants with practical strategies to motivate individuals, resolve issues, and unify the team.

To schedule one of these seminars or to have your specific needs addressed, please contact us.

Redmond Leadership Institute
PO Box 703052
Tulsa, Oklahoma 74170

918.298.7766

Contact @ redmondleadership.org

CD SEMINARS

The Wealth Creation School

The *Wealth Creation School* is a perfect complement to the *Power to Create* curriculum! What are the most effective drivers of wealth? What are the eight powerful strategies for moving from scarcity to abundance? These and many other key questions are answered in this CD School.

The Leadership School

Don't miss out on Tim's *Leadership School*! Many have reported boosted confidence, improved resolution skills, and clearer vision as a result of going through this leadership package. One executive recently stated it was the best leadership training he has heard.

To obtain these CD packages, go to www.PowerToCreate.org, or call us at 918.298.7766.

Relationships & Finances Kit

Tim and Sandy share valuable lessons from their heart-touching experiences contained in this CD package. Marriages have been healed and strengthened. Decision-making has become much smoother—especially regarding finances and investments.

To obtain these CD packages, go to www.PowerToCreate.org, or call us at 918.298.7766.

ACCELERATED GROWTH COACHING PROGRAM

 Tap into Tim's 25 years of business growth expertise. He has helped countless business people, pastors, and leaders significantly grow their organizations even in challenging economic times. One business owner who became a member reported 43 percent growth last year and 119 percent growth this year!

Each month, Tim trains on crucial growth topics covering the world's best practices, mindsets, and strategies via computer or phone. As part of each session, get your specific questions answered "live" by Tim—a service that others pay thousands for.

If you can't make the live training session or want to review it later, no problem! The webinar and recordings will be available soon after each session. Tim also makes available the Training Manuals that include his valuable research notes, references, links to thought-provoking articles, application tools, and motivating quotes and scriptures.

If you are interested in a more advanced program with even better results, ask about the *Platinum Accelerated Growth Coaching Program*.

To enroll or for more information, go to www.PowerToCreate.org, email us at contact@redmondleadership.org, or call us at 918.298.7766.